D1091537

e Series OCT 1 7 1984

No. 269   FOREIGN POLICY ASSOCIATION $3.00

THE TWO

KOREAS

by Bruce Cumings

Cover Design: Hersch Wartik   May/June 1984

The Author

BRUCE CUMINGS has followed Korean affairs since serving there in the Peace Corps in the late 1960s. He is a graduate of Denison University, with an M.A. from Indiana University and a Ph.D. in political science and East Asian studies from Columbia University. He taught at Swarthmore College, and then joined the faculty of the Jackson School of International Studies at the University of Washington, where he is associate professor. He lived in South Korea for more than two years and visited North Korea in 1981. From 1977 to 1979 he coedited the *Bulletin of Concerned Asian Scholars* and now coedits *The Journal of Korean Studies*. He served on the Korea Committee of the Social Science Research Council for five years. His book, *The Origins of the Korean War*, was co-winner of the Harry S Truman Award in 1982 and won the John Fairbank Award of the American Historical Association in 1983.

The Foreign Policy Association

The Foreign Policy Association is a private, nonprofit, nonpartisan educational organization. Its purpose is to stimulate wider interest and more effective participation in, and greater understanding of, world affairs among American citizens. Among its activities is the continuous publication, dating from 1935, of the HEADLINE SERIES. The author is responsible for factual accuracy and for the views expressed. FPA itself takes no position on issues of U.S. foreign policy.

HEADLINE SERIES (ISSN 0017-8780) is published five times a year, January, March, May, September and November, by the Foreign Policy Association, Inc., 205 Lexington Ave., New York, N.Y. 10016. Chairman, Leonard H. Marks; President, Archie E. Albright; Editor, Nancy L. Hoepli; Associate Editors, Ann R. Monjo and Mary E. Stavrou. Subscription rates, $12.00 for 5 issues; $20.00 for 10 issues; $28.00 for 15 issues. Single copy price $3.00. Discount 25% on 10 to 99 copies; 30% on 100 to 499; 35% on 500 to 999; 40% on 1,000 or more. Payment must accompany order for $6 or less. Second-class postage paid at New York, N.Y. POSTMASTER: Send address changes to HEADLINE SERIES, Foreign Policy Association, 205 Lexington Ave., New York, N.Y. 10016. Copyright 1984 by Foreign Policy Association, Inc. Composed and printed at Science Press, Ephrata, Pa.

Library of Congress Catalog No. 84-81643
ISBN 0-87124-092-0

Introduction

Imagine a country roughly the shape of New Jersey and the size of Minnesota, with the difference that over 60 million people live there. Then imagine that this country had a more devastating civil war than our own, 34 years ago rather than a century ago, and that this civil war never ended. The northern and southern sides retained their separate states, the union was not accomplished, and both sides immediately rearmed to fight or deter another war. Conjure up a present in which more than a million soldiers confront each other across a Mason-Dixon line, armed to the teeth with the latest equipment; the line is so firm that nothing crosses it, not even mail between divided families.

Now factor into this situation the great divide of the postwar period between communism and capitalism, and make the north Communist and the south capitalist. Surround this country with four big powers. These powers pour in billions of dollars of economic and military support to each side. Last, put 40,000 young American soldiers, the latest fighter-bombers, a multitude of military bases, and at least 250 tactical nuclear weapons into the south; then surround it with an array of naval forces. Back up the north with the two biggest Communist powers.

An impossible situation, one might think. Yet this is Korea in 1984. Here is North Korea in a New Year's message to the U.S. government: "The present situation is strained so extremely that an accidental trifling incident might trigger off a war at any minute . . . [A new war] would inevitably expand into a nuclear war."

Because Korea remains a cold-war island (or peninsula) in post-cold-war Northeast Asia, it is appropriate to remind readers of the continuing danger of war. But one does so at the risk of conjuring up an old, misleading image: Korea, the war-torn, helpless mendicant of the 1950s. The traveler to the two Koreas today could not imagine the devastation of 1953. In Seoul, capital of South Korea, one would be overwhelmed by the shimmering skyscrapers, the bustling citizenry, the raw dynamism of one of the world's most rapidly industrializing countries. In the North Korean capital, Pyongyang, one would see wide boulevards, beautiful parks, and a society of workaholics also fully devoted to economic development. Both Koreas would seem to be success stories of modernization, but on entirely different models. So, one comes to another image: world-beating, rapid economic development that has transformed the face of old Korea in one generation. How can one explain this outcome, which no one could have predicted in 1953? In Korea, best-case capitalism seems to be meeting best-case socialism, at least in terms of third-world economic growth.

In politics, however, there is a third image: worst-case socialism meets worst-case capitalism. In recent years South Korea has become a symbol of authoritarian politics and human rights violations, while North Korea is a leading favorite for that society most resembling George Orwell's *1984*. Both are severely lacking in those attributes dear to the heart of Western liberalism. However, in probing beneath these stereotypes two interesting political systems may be discerned, however repellent either may be from a liberal standpoint. Both systems are a mixture of Western concepts and authoritarian Korean political experience, which encompassed few if any democratic freedoms of the Western kind.

It is perhaps Korea's position in the international system that makes a reconsideration of the two Koreas most important and timely. It is such an anomalous position. As if it were still 1953, the United States backs the South and the U.S.S.R. and China back the North, and none of the big powers has diplomatic relations with both Koreas. Yet the international environment surrounding Korea has changed dramatically: China and the United States are friends; China and the U.S.S.R. have recently been enemies and remain hostile to each other; Japan has diplomatic relations with and trades widely with all the other big powers. Since 1972 it has seemed that the changed external environment would effect corresponding internal changes on the Korean peninsula. That has not yet happened, but it is quite likely that it will happen during the 1980s.

It is particularly important and urgent for Americans to learn about, or deepen their knowledge of, the two Koreas. The United States has an enormous responsibility for the state of the Korean peninsula today, a military role that could make it a belligerent in any new war overnight, and a rapidly increasing trade with the Republic of Korea (ROK) in the south. If Americans fail to comprehend their past and present role in Korea, they do so at their peril, for Korea in the postwar period has had a knack for forcibly bringing itself to our attention.

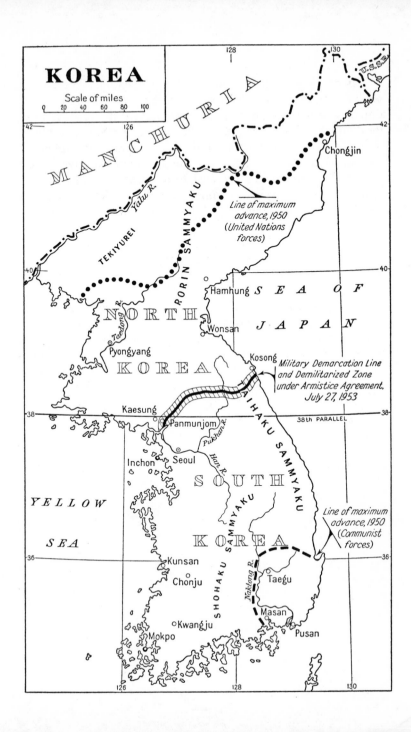

1

Traditional Legacies

The two Koreas, like many other developing countries, are often termed "new nations." That there are two of them, both "new," would be incomprehensible to any Korean of the old order that died in 1910. Why? Because Korea in 1910 had two remarkable characteristics: an ancient nation, a unitary nation. Korea's recorded history extends back before the birth of Christ; its unitary existence dates from the seventh century A.D. It had many of the requisites of nationhood—political unity, common language, ethnic homogeneity, well-recognized international boundaries—long before the nations of Europe emerged. Indeed, Korea is one of the few nations in the world where ethnic and linguistic unity coincide exactly with national boundaries (Japan is another). Relatively few Koreans live outside Korea, and the only minority within Korea is a small Chinese community. Linguistic and dialect differences are minor and of no conse-

Map from *Korea: A Study of U.S. Policy in the United Nations*, by Leland M. Goodrich, © Council on Foreign Relations. Reprinted in 1979 by Greenwood Press, Inc.

quence. Thus the period of national division since 1945 is not only a very small parenthesis within centuries of unity, but also a sharp wound to the pride of a people with a long and dignified history of self-rule. Korea's experience differs sharply from that of another divided country, Germany: the latter's unity is little more than a century old, and the territory of Germany was laced with ethnic and linguistic variations. So, it is divided Korea that is the anomaly, and therefore reconciliation and reunion have been and will remain the overriding goal of most Koreans.

A tradition as long and proud as Korea's has other legacies for the present, however, and the important ones may be summarized under the following rubrics: (1) Confucian residues; (2) *yangbans* (aristocrats) and commoners; (3) scholars and landlords; (4) agrarian bureaucracy; (5) stability and continuity in politics; and (6) benign neglect within the Chinese world order.

Confucian Residues

When the Yi Dynasty replaced the old Koryo Dynasty (from which we get the name Korea) in 1392, it inaugurated a more than 500-year period of Confucian statecraft that did not end until 1910. By the late 19th century, Korea seemed so suffused with Confucian doctrine that foreign travelers termed it "more Confucian than China." This was an exaggeration that overlooked the many innovations and differences in the Korean brand, but nonetheless the Confucian heritage has unquestionably stamped Korea as indelibly as it did China. It remains a powerful influence today.

Confucianism, the moral and religious system based on the teachings of Confucius, began with the family and an ideal model of relations between family members. It then generalized this family model to the state, and to an international system (the Chinese world order). The principle was hierarchy within a reciprocal web of duties and obligations: the son obeyed the father by following the dictates of filial piety; the father provided for and educated the son. Daughters obeyed mothers, younger siblings followed older siblings, wives were subordinate to husbands. The superior prestige and privileges of older adults made longevity a

Confucianism is a powerful legacy in the two Koreas. In Seoul, the birthday of Confucius is observed with music played on traditional Chinese-style instruments.

prime virtue. Generalized to politics, a village followed the leadership of venerated elders, and citizens revered a king or emperor who was thought of as the father of the state. Generalized to international affairs, the Chinese emperor was the big brother of the Korean king.

The glue holding the system together was education, meaning socialization into Confucian norms and virtues that began in early childhood with the reading of the Confucian classics. The model figure was the "true gentleman," the virtuous and learned scholar who was equally adept at poetry or statecraft. In China, even the poorest families would seek to spare one son from work in the fields so that he could study for state-run exams. If he passed, it would bring him an official position and, it was hoped, transform the situation of the rest of the family. Students had to learn the extraordinarily difficult classical Chinese language, meaning mastery of thousands of written characters and their many meanings; rote memorization was the typical method. In Korea, this meant that throughout the Yi Dynasty all official records, all formal education, and most written discourse was in classical Chinese. (The fascinating, scientific Korean written alphabet was systematized in the 15th century under that greatest of Korean kings, Sejong, but it did not come into general use until the 20th century; today the North Koreans use the Korean alphabet exclusively, while the South Koreans retain a mixed Sino-Korean script.) With this Chinese language came a profound cultural penetration of Korea, such that most Korean arts and literature came to use Chinese models.

Confucianism is often thought to be a conservative philosophy, stressing tradition, veneration of a past golden age, careful attention to the performance of ritual, obedience to superiors, disdain for material things, commerce, and the remaking of nature, and a preference for relatively frozen hierarchies. Much commentary on contemporary South Korea focuses on the alleged authoritarian, antidemocratic character of this Confucian legacy. Yet one-sided emphasis on these aspects would never explain the extraordinary commercial bustle of South Korea, the materialism and conspicuous consumption of new elites, or the determined struggles for democratization put up by Korean college students. At the same time, the assumption that North Korean communism broke completely with the past would blind one to continuing Confucian legacies there: family-based politics, the succession to rule of the leader's son, and the extraordinary veneration of Kim Il Sung, North Korea's leader since 1946.

Perhaps the most persistent legacies of the old Confucian order are the emphasis on the family and the remarkable attention paid to education. Seoul's population has long had the highest percentage of students of any city in the world; North Korea runs campaigns to make everyone "an intellectual." Families interpenetrate the biggest corporations and the state executive in the

South; they interpenetrate the Central Committee in the North. If something survives communism in one half and capitalism in the other, it must be important.

Yangbans and Commoners

The Yi Dynasty (1392–1910) had a traditional class structure that departed from the Chinese Confucian example, thus providing another important legacy for the modern period. Korea had a landed aristocracy mingled with a Confucian-educated stratum of scholar-officials; often scholars and landlords were one and the same person, but in any case landed wealth and bureaucratic position were powerfully fused. Yangban is the Korean term for this aristocracy; its key features were its possession of land, its monopoly on education and official positions, and its requirement of hereditary lineage for entry to yangban status.

Unlike the situation in China, commoners could not sit for state-run examinations leading to official positions. One had to prove that one belonged to a yangban family, which in practice meant a forebear having sat for exams within the past four generations. In Korea as in China, of course, the majority of peasant families could not spare a son to study for the exams anyway, so that upward social mobility was sharply limited in both societies. But in Korea the limit was specifically hereditary as well, leading to less mobility than in China. A major study of all exam-passers in the Yi Dynasty (some 14,000) showed remarkable continuity among elite families producing students to sit for the exams; other studies have documented the persistence of this pattern into the early 20th century. Even in 1945 one can say that this aristocracy was substantially intact, although its effective demise came soon after.

Korea's traditional class system also included a majority who were peasants, and minorities of petty clerks, merchants, and so-called "base" classes, caste-like hereditary groups such as butchers, leather tanners, and beggars. Korea had no military tradition comparable to Japan's with its samurai or warlord aristocracy, although Koreans revere military leaders who defeated foreign invasions—ones like Yi Sun-shin, whose armor-

11

clad "turtle" ships and sophisticated naval warfare helped hold off the Japanese during invasions in the 1590s, or Ulchi Mundok, who led a successful defense of Korea against one of the rare Chinese attacks in 612 A.D.

Class and status hierarchies also were built into the Korean language, so that one addresses superiors and inferiors quite differently, and elders can only be spoken to using elaborate honorifics. Even verb endings and conjugations will differ. Here Korean is closer to Japanese than to Chinese; the studied formalism of hierarchical language has declined, but about four or five levels of hierarchy remain in common spoken discourse today. The egalitarian emphases of North Korea have lessened but by no means ended this pattern: there are, for example, two terms for "comrade," depending on whether the person is an honored comrade or just a regular one.

Scholars and Landlords

The fusion of official position and landed wealth created an aristocracy of long standing, such that a family prominent in 1620 might also be prominent in 1920. The traditional emphasis on landholding and Confucian education combined to make the yangban literati gentlemen and statesmen at best, but effete, ineffectual, undynamic types at worst. Early Western travelers to Korea were of course full of their own biases, expecting to find an indolent East to contrast with a "dynamic" West; still, when compared to the writings on Japan and China during the same period, this literature reeks of disdain for an old Korean ruling class that seemed to foreigners to be exploitative, parasitic, and above all incapable of invigorating Korea effectively to resist the foreign impact. Believers in a philosophy that renounced material pursuits and disdained the accumulation (or at least reinvestment) of wealth, and that valued the lettered man over the enterprising man, Korean scholar-officials returned foreign disdain with their own healthy contempt for the new Western learning. In so doing they weakened Korea internally, so that its resistance to the imperial onslaught of the late 19th century was ineffectual and ended in the catastrophe of colonial rule and national oblivion. The persistence of the yangban, clinging to the traditional culture into the late 19th century, was thus one of the reasons for Korea's faltering response to the Western challenge, in sharp contrast to Japan's response.

Korea's scholar-landlords also presided over a land situation of widespread tenancy and penury, and relatively little agrarian progress. Non-entrepreneurial themselves, they also inhibited the formation of wealth among richer peasants. Again, the contrast with Japanese agrarian change in the premodern period is pronounced. At the same time, Confucian dislike for business and scholar-official monopolies attenuated Korea's commercial impulse. The very depth of Korean Confucianism, its long-term persistence as an aspect of aristocratic rule, left Korea in the late 19th century without a growing agrarian or urban commerce, without a strong military, without much interest in or tolerance for the new Western learning, and therefore without many resources for resisting the persistent imperial attentions of the West. Scholar-officials and landlords were not enough.

Agrarian Bureaucracy

Koreans today describe the traditional system and its contemporary holdovers as "feudal." But one cannot call the Yi Dynasty feudal. Why not? Because—again unlike Japan, but like China—it did not betray the classic characteristics of feudalism, such as local, fragmented sovereignty, a martial spirit and a military caste or class, rural domains with autonomous lords and their vassals. So what should the traditional system be called? The best term is agrarian bureaucracy.

It was bureaucratic because it possessed an elaborate procedure for entry to the highly structured civil service and a practice of administering the country from the top down and from the center. Thus, unlike a feudal system, Korea had strong central administration that ruled through a civilian bureaucracy, not through lords who fused civil and military functions. Once again there is a Chinese model behind Korean practice, in this case the Confucian bureaucratic system, but Korea nonetheless departed significantly from the Chinese experience.

The system rested upon an agrarian base, making it different from modern bureaucratic systems; the particular character of agrarian-bureaucratic interaction also provided one of Korea's departures from the typical Chinese experience. The premier historian of the Yi Dynasty, James B. Palais, has shown that conflict between bureaucrats seeking revenues for government coffers and landowners hoping to control tenants and harvests was a constant during the dynasty, and that in this conflict over resources the landowners often won out. Landed power was stronger and more persistent than in China. Korea had centralized administration, to be sure, but the center was more often a facade concealing the reality of aristocratic power. The state ostensibly dominated the society, but in fact landed aristocratic families could keep the state at bay and perpetuate local power for centuries. This pattern persisted until the late 1940s, when landed dominance was obliterated in a northern revolution and attenuated in southern land reform; since that time the balance has shifted toward strong central power and top-down administration in both North and South Korea.

Stability and Persistence

Following Korea's opening to the West and Japan in 1876, the Yi Dynasty faltered and then collapsed in a few decades. What accounts for its 500-year span, which included devastating invasions by the Japanese and the Manchus?

In essence the traditional system was adaptable, even supple in the marginal adjustments and incremental responses necessary to forestall or accommodate domestic or internal conflict and change, but it could not withstand the full foreign onslaught of technically advanced imperial powers with strong armies. Dr. Palais has shown that the old agrarian bureaucracy managed the interplay of different and competing interests by having a system of checks and balances that tended over time to equilibrate the interests of different parties. The king and the bureaucracy kept watch on each other, the royal clans watched both, scholars could criticize ("remonstrate") from the superior moral position of Confucian doctrine, secret inspectors and censors went around the country to watch for rebellion and assure accurate reporting, landed aristocrats sent sons into the bureaucracy to protect family interests and local potentates influenced county magistrates sent down from the central administration. The centralized facade masked a dispersal of power, sets of competing interests, and institutional checks and balances that prevented one group from getting all that there was to get. The Yi Dynasty was not a system that modern Koreans would wish to restore or live under, but in its time it was a sophisticated political system, adaptable enough and persistent enough to give unified rule to Korea for half a millennium.

Many features of this traditional system persist in Korea today. In the South, county leaders are moved very frequently from post to post so that they do not become too responsive to local concerns and forget the center. In North Korea, Kim Il Sung frequently castigates the "bureaucratism" of officials who put on airs, send inadequate or false reports to the center, or fail both to remember the policies of the center and the necessity to explain them patiently and adapt them to differing local situations. He has even been known to send secret inspectors to watch local bureaucratic performance. Both Koreas also know how to preserve central power. South Korea's Park Chung Hee ruled for 18 years against much opposition, and was only removed by an assassin. Kim Il Sung has ruled in the North de facto from February 1946 to the present; in the postwar world only Enver Hoxha of Albania has ruled for a longer period.

Benign Neglect

Korean states have always had to work out their fate amidst big-power conflict; Koreans for good reason tend to view foreign powers as predatory and up to no good. All Koreans dislike Japan for terminating Korean independence in 1910. South Koreans revile the Soviet Union, and North Koreans revile the United States. But China is an exception. For centuries Korea lived within the Chinese world order. Chinese arts, letters, language, philosophy and bureaucratic practice radiated outward from the "Middle Kingdom" to tributary states. This was a cultural universe that defined civilization by closeness to the Chinese source. Korea was China's little brother, a model tributary state, and in many ways the most important of China's allies. Koreans revered things Chinese, and China responded by being for the most part a good neighbor, giving more than it took. Exercising a light-handed suzerainty over Korea and assuming that enlightened Koreans would follow China without being forced, absolutely convinced of its own superiority, China indulged in a policy that might be called benign neglect of things Korean, thereby allowing Korea substantive autonomy as a nation.

This sophisticated world order was broken up and laid low by the Western impact in the late 19th century. As a small power, Korea had to learn to be shrewd in foreign policy, and it had a good example in China. Koreans cultivated the sophisticated art of "low determines high" diplomacy, seeking to use foreign power for their own ends, wagging the dog with its tail. Thus both South Korea and North Korea strike foreign observers as rather dependent on big-power support, yet both not only claim but strongly assert their absolute autonomy and independence as nation-states, and both are adept at manipulating their big-power backers. North Korea may have a bizarre and heavy-handed internal system, but it has been masterful both in getting big powers to fight its battles (South Korea has done well here, too) and in maneuvering between the two Communist giants to get something from each and to prevent either from dominating it. Much like the traditional period, North Korea's heart is with China (even though its head is sometimes with the U.S.S.R., when it needs technology and weaponry); China, unlike any other foreign power, is not criticized in the press, and Kim Il Sung occasionally diverts himself with secret trips to share vacations with Chinese leaders. In the past decade South Korea, too, has sought relations with China; in spite of China's belligerent status in the Korean War, many South Koreans remember the good discipline of Chinese soldiers, something that reinforced the Korean tendency to view China as a special case amongst foreigners.

The soft spot that Koreans have in their hearts for China should not blind anyone to the main characteristic of Korea's traditional diplomacy: isolationism, even what historian Dr. Kim

Key-Hiuk has called exclusionism. For 300 years after the Japanese invasions of the 1590s Korea isolated itself from Japan, dealt harshly with errant Westerners washing up on its shores, and kept the Chinese at arm's length. Thus Westerners called Korea the Hermit Kingdom, describing the pronounced streak of obstinate hostility toward foreign power and the deep desire for independence that marked traditional Korea. A self-contained, autonomous Korea not besmirched by things foreign remains an ideal for many Koreans. North Korea has exercised a "hermit kingdom" option by remaining one of the more isolated states in the world (and not just from the West: villages in the border area have signs exhorting citizens to watch out for Chinese and Soviet spies!), and it is really South Korea that, since 1960, has been revolutionary in the Korean context by pursuing an open-door policy toward the world market and seeking a multilateral, varied diplomacy. Calls for self-reliance and expelling foreign influence will always get a hearing in Korea; this is one of its most persistent foreign policy traits.

2

The Colonial Pressure Cooker

In 1905 Japan capped several decades of imperial rivalry in Northeast Asia by defeating Russia in war and establishing a protectorate over Korea; President Theodore Roosevelt aided the negotiations that brought this result, and the United States did not challenge Japanese control of Korea. Japan completed its seizure of Korea by annexing it in 1910 and putting an end to the Yi Dynasty. Korea only escaped the Japanese grip in 1945, when Japan lay prostrate after the American and Russian onslaught brought World War II to a close. This colonial experience was intense and bitter and affected postwar Korea deeply. It led to development and underdevelopment; agrarian growth and increased tenancy; industrialization and extraordinary dislocation; political mobilization and deactivation; a new role for a strong state; new sets of Korean political leaders; communism and nationalism; armed resistance and treacherous collaboration. It left deep fissures and conflicts that have gnawed at the Korean national identity ever since.

Colonialism is often thought to have created new nations where none existed before, to bring diverse tribes and peoples together, draw national boundaries, tutor the natives in self-government, and prepare for the day when the imperial power decides to grant independence. But all of this existed in Korea for centuries before 1910. Furthermore, by virtue of their relative closeness to China, Koreans had always felt superior to Japan and blamed Japan's devastating 16th-century invasions for hindering Korean wealth and power in subsequent centuries.

Thus the Japanese engaged not in creation but in substitution after 1910: substituting a Japanese ruling elite for the Korean yangban scholar-officials, Japanese modern education for Confucian classics, Japanese capital and expertise for the budding Korean versions, imperial coordination for the traditional bureaucracy, Japanese talent for Korean talent, and eventually even the Japanese language for Korean. Koreans never thanked the Japanese for these substitutions, did not credit Japan with creations, and instead saw Japan as snatching away the *ancien régime,* Korea's sovereignty and independence, its indigenous if incipient modernization, and above all its national dignity. Unlike some other colonial peoples, therefore, Koreans never saw Japanese rule as anything but illegitimate and humiliating. Furthermore, the very closeness of the two nations—in geography, in common Chinese cultural influences, indeed in levels of development until the 19th century—made Japanese dominance all the more galling to the Koreans. It gave a peculiar intensity to the relationship, a love/hate dynamic that suggested to Koreans, "there but for accidents of history go we," and that periodically caused revolts against the Japanese. The biggest was in 1919.

The Strong State

The Japanese built bureaucracies in Korea, all of them centralized and all of them big by colonial standards. Unlike, say, the relatively small British colonial cadre in India, the Japanese came in large numbers (700,000 by the 1940s), and the majority of colonizers worked in government service. For the first time in history Korea had a national police, responsive to the center and possessing its own communication and transportation facilities. The huge Oriental Development Company organized and funded industrial and agricultural projects and came to own more than 20 percent of Korea's arable land; it employed an army of officials who fanned out through the countryside to supervise agricultural production. The official Bank of Korea performed central banking functions, such as regulating interest rates, and provided credit to entrepreneurs—almost all of them, of course, Japanese. Central judicial bodies wrote new laws establishing an extensive, "legalized" system of racial discrimination against Koreans, making them second-class citizens in their own country. Bureaucratic departments proliferated at the Government-General headquarters in Seoul, turning it into the nerve center of the country. Semi-official companies and conglomerates, including the big *zaibatsu* (Japanese cartels) such as Mitsubishi and Mitsui, laid railways, built ports, installed modern factories and, in fine, remade the face of old Korea.

Japan held Korea tightly, watched it closely, and pursued an organized colonialism in which the planner and administrator, not a swashbuckling conqueror, was the model. The strong, highly centralized colonial state mimicked the role that the Japanese state had come to play in Japan—intervening in the economy, creating markets, spawning new industries, suppressing dissent. Politically, Koreans could barely breathe, but economically there was substantial, if unevenly distributed, growth. Agricultural output rose significantly in the 1920s, and a "hothouse" industrialization developed in the 1930s. Growth rates in the Korean economy often outstripped those in Japan; recent research has suggested an annual economic growth rate for Korea of 3.5 percent in the period 1911–38, a rate of 3.4 percent for Japan.

Koreans have always thought that the benefits of this growth went entirely to Japan, and that Korea would have developed rapidly anyway, without Japanese help. Nevertheless, the strong colonial state, the multiplicity of bureaucracies, the policy of administrative guidance of the economy, the use of the state to found new industries, and the repression of labor unions and dissidents that always went with it provided a model for both Koreas after World War II. Japan showed them an early version of the "bureaucratic-authoritarian" path to industrialization, and it was a lesson that seemed well learned by the 1970s.

Political Elites and Political Fissures

The colonial period brought forth an entirely new set of Korean political leaders, spawned both by the resistance to and the opportunities of Japanese colonialism. The emergence of nationalist and Communist groups dates back to the 1920s; it is really in this period that the left–right splits of postwar Korea began. The transformation of the yangban aristocracy also began then. In the 1930s new groups of armed resisters, bureaucrats, and, for the first time, military leaders emerged. Both North and South Korea remain profoundly influenced by political elites and political conflicts generated during colonial rule.

One thing from the Yi Dynasty that the Japanese did not destroy was the yangban aristocracy. The higher scholar-officials who did not leave on their own were pensioned off and replaced by Japanese, but many landlords were allowed to retain their holdings and encouraged to continue disciplining peasants and extracting rice. The traditional landholding system was put on a new legal basis, but tenancy continued and became more entrenched throughout the colonial period; by 1945 Korea had an agricultural tenancy system with few parallels in the world. While more-traditional landlords were content to sit back and let Japanese officials increase output (by 1945 such people were widely viewed as treacherous collaborators with the Japanese), beginning in the 1920s other landlords were becoming entrepreneurs.

The more-enlightened and entrepreneurial landlords were able to diversify their wealth, investing in industries (often textiles), banks, newspapers, and schools. A good example was Kim Song-su, who owned the largest Korean textile mill, founded what is now Korea University, and owned the leading Korean-language newspaper. Much of this activity was justified as the creation of Korean "national capital," and as a form of moderate nationalism and resistance to the Japanese. This group is the basis of much of the top political leadership in postwar South Korea; Kim Song-su and his associates founded and led the Korean Democratic party after 1945, provided many officials during the American occupation (1945–48), and then structured the moderate opposition to the regime of President Syngman Rhee (1948–60).

Many younger Koreans, after the massive March 1, 1919, independence demonstrations were put down fiercely by the Japanese, became militant opponents of colonial rule. Some went into exile in China and the U.S.S.R. and founded early Communist and nationalist resistance groups. A Korean Communist party (KCP) was founded in Korea in 1925; a man named Pak Hon-yong was one of the organizers, and he became a leader of Korean communism in Korea after 1945. Various nationalist groups also emerged during this period, including the exiled Korean Provisional Government (KPG) in Shanghai, which included Syngman Rhee among its members.

Police repression and internal factionalism made it impossible for these groups to sustain themselves over time. Many nationalist and Communist leaders were thrown in jail in the early 1930s, only to emerge in 1945. When Japan invaded and then annexed Manchuria in 1931, however, a strong guerrilla resistance embracing Chinese and Koreans emerged in Sino-Korean border areas. There may have been as many as 200,000 guerrillas (all loosely connected, and including bandits and secret societies) fighting the Japanese in the early 1930s; after murderous but effective counterinsurgency campaigns, the numbers declined to a few thousand by the mid-1930s. It was in this milieu that Kim Il Sung (originally named Kim Song-ju) emerged. He was a significant guerrilla leader by the mid-1930s and was considered among the most effective and dangerous of guerrillas by the Japanese in the late 1930s. They formed a special counterinsurgent unit to track Kim down and put Koreans in it as part of their divide-and-rule tactics.

There are ridiculous myths about this guerrilla resistance in both Koreas today: the North claiming that Kim single-handedly defeated the Japanese, and the South claiming that Kim is an imposter who stole the name of the revered patriot. Nonetheless, this experience is important for an understanding of postwar Korea. The resistance to the Japanese is the main legitimating doctrine of the Democratic People's Republic of Korea (DPRK);

North Korea's friendship with China, forged in the early 1930s, was strengthened by North Korean President Kim Il Sung's visit to Beijing in 1975. He was welcomed by Chinese Vice Premier Deng Xiaoping.

they trace the origin of the army, the leadership, and their ideology back to that period. Even today the top North Korean leadership is still dominated, as it has been since 1946, by a core group that fought the Japanese in Manchuria.

Japan attacked China in 1937 and the United States in 1941, and as this war took on global proportions, Koreans for the first time had military careers opened to them. Although most were conscripted foot soldiers, a small number achieved officer status and a few even attained high rank. Virtually the entire officer corps of the ROK army during the Syngman Rhee period was drawn from Koreans with experience in the Japanese army. Lower-ranking officers also were prominent during the Park Chung Hee period, including Park himself, who had been a lieutenant in the Japanese army. At least in part, the Korean War was a matter of Japanese-trained military officers fighting Japanese-spawned resistance leaders.

Japan's far-flung war effort also caused a labor shortage throughout the empire. In Korea this meant that jobs in the bureaucracy were more available to Koreans than at any previous time; thus a substantial cadre of Koreans got experience in government, local administration, police and judicial work, economic planning agencies, banks, and the like. That this occurred in the last decade of colonialism created a divisive legacy, however, for this was also the harshest period of Japanese rule, the time Koreans remember with greatest bitterness. Koreans were required to speak Japanese and to take Japanese names. The majority suffered badly at the precise time that a minority was doing well; this minority acquired the taint of collaboration and never successfully shucked it off. Korea from 1937 to 1945 was much like Vichy France in the early 1940s: bitter experiences and memories continue to divide people, even within the same family; it is too painful to confront directly, and so it amounts now to buried history. Nonetheless, it continues to play upon the national identity.

With a Bang, Not a Whimper

Perhaps the most important characteristic of Korea's colonial experience was the manner in which it ended: the last decade of a four-decade imperium was a pressure cooker, building up tensions that exploded in the postwar period. Industrialization, in particular, both developed and deformed Korean society.

Japan in the mid-1930s entered a phase of heavy industrialization that embraced all of Northeast Asia. Unlike most colonial powers, Japan located heavy industry in its colonies, bringing the means of production to the labor and raw materials. Manchuria and northern Korea got steel mills, auto plants, petrochemical complexes, enormous hydroelectric facilities; the region was held exclusively by Japan and tied together with the home market to the degree that national boundaries became less important than the new transnational, integrated production. To facilitate this production, Japan also built railroads, highways, cities, ports, and other instruments of modern transportation and communication. By 1945 Korea proportionally had more railroad miles than any other Asian country save Japan, leaving only remote parts of the central east coast and the wild northeastern Sino-Korean border region untouched by modern means of conveyance. These changes had been externally induced and served Japanese, not Korean, interests. Thus they represented a kind of overdevelopment.

The same changes fostered underdevelopment in Korean society as a whole. Since the changes were not indigenous, the Korean upper and managerial classes did not blossom; instead their development was retarded. Amongst the majority peasant class, change was pronounced. Koreans became the mobile human resource used to work the new factories in northern Korea and Manchuria, mines and other enterprises in Japan, and urban factories in southern Korea. Between 1935 and 1945 Korea began its industrial revolution, with many of the usual characteristics: uprooting of peasants from the land, the emergence of a working class, urbanization, and population mobility. In Korea the process was telescoped, giving rise to remarkable population movements. By 1945 about 11 percent of the entire Korean population was abroad (mostly in Japan and Manchuria), and fully 20 percent of all Koreans were either abroad or in a province other than that in which they were born (with most of the interprovincial movement being southern peasants moving into northern industry). This was, by and large, a forced or mobilized movement; by 1942 it was even conscripted labor. Peasants lost land or rights to work land only to end up working in unfamiliar factory settings for a pittance.

When the colonial system abruptly terminated in 1945, millions of Koreans sought to return to their native villages from these far-flung mobilization details. But they were no longer the same people: they had grievances against those who remained secure at home, they had suffered material and status losses, they had often come into contact with new ideologies, they had all seen a broader world beyond the villages. It was thus this pressure cooker of a final decade that loosed upon postwar Korea a mass of disgruntled and changed people who created deep disorder in the liberation period and the plans of the Americans and the Soviets.

3

Liberation,
Separate Regimes, War

The crucible of the period of national division and rival regimes that still remains in Korea was the decade from 1943 to 1953. Nothing about the politics of contemporary Korea can be understood without comprehending the events of this decade. It was the breeding ground of the two Koreas, of war, and of a reordering of international politics in Northeast Asia.

The important dates of this period would seem to be 1945, when American and Soviet forces moved into Korea to accept the Japanese surrender; 1948, when each sponsored the separate emergence of the ROK and the DPRK; and June 1950, when the Korean War began. A different dating helps to elucidate some underlying themes, however: the critical years here would be 1943, 1947 and 1950 (October) for the United States, 1946 and 1949 for the Soviets, 1946 for the two Koreas.

American Policy, 1943–50

The United States took the initiative in big-power deliberations on Korea during World War II, suggesting a multilateral trusteeship for postwar Korea to the British in March 1943, and to the Soviets at the end of the same year. President Franklin D. Roosevelt, worried about the disposition of enemy-held colonial territories and aware of colonial demands for independence, sought a gradualist policy of preparing colonials (like the Koreans) for self-government and independence. He knew that since Korea touched the Soviet border, the Russians would want to be involved in the fate of postwar Korea; he hoped to get a Soviet commitment to a multilateral administration to forestall unilateral solutions and provide an entry for American interests in Korea. At about the same time, planners in the State Department drastically altered traditional U.S. policy toward Korea by defining the security of the peninsula as important to the security of the postwar Pacific, which was in turn very important to American security. It was this early planning that reflected a new-found U.S. interest in Korea, and that lay behind the American decision to send troops to Korea in 1945.

The period 1943 to 1947 was an internationalist phase in U.S. diplomacy, reflected in the trusteeship policy and the U.S. desire to place a still-unified Korea under temporary multilateral administration. At least this was how State Department planners in Washington viewed Korea. Yet when 25,000 American soldiers occupied southern Korea in early September 1945, they found themselves up against a strong Korean impulse for independence and for thorough reform of colonial legacies. By and large Koreans wished to solve their problems themselves and resented any inference that they were not ready for self-government. The American military command, along with emissaries dispatched from Washington, tended to view this resistance as radical and pro-Soviet. When Korean resistance leaders set up an interim "People's Republic" and so-called people's committees throughout southern Korea in September 1945, the United States interpreted a fundamentally indigenous movement as part of a Soviet master plan to dominate all of Korea. Radical activity, such as the ousting of landlords and attacks on Koreans in the colonial police, was usually a matter of settling scores left over from the colonial period, or of quite legitimate demands by Koreans to run their own affairs. But it immediately became wrapped up with

Soviet-American rivalry, such that the cold war arrived early in Korea—really in the last months of 1945.

By 1947 Washington was willing to acknowledge formally the existence of the cold war and abandoned attempts to work with the Soviets toward a multilateral administration in Korea. Recently declassified documents show that when President Harry S Truman announced the Truman Doctrine which inaugurated the containment policy in the spring of 1947, Korea was very nearly included along with Greece and Turkey as a key country to be "contained" from Soviet advances; State Department planners foresaw a whopping $600 million package of economic and military aid for southern Korea, only abandoning it when Congress and the War Department balked at such a huge sum. Instead the decision was made to seek United Nations backing for U.S. policy in Korea, and to hold UN-sponsored elections in all of Korea if the Soviets would go along, in southern Korea alone if they did not. The elections were then held in May 1948, and they resulted in the establishment of the ROK in August of the same year.

Thus 1947 was the key year in which formal U.S. policy moved from multilateral internationalism to unilateral containment in Korea. There were at this time severe global limits on U.S. power, and the Truman Administration could not publicly commit arms and money to Korea on the same scale as to Greece and Turkey. But in secret congressional testimony in early 1947, Dean Acheson said that we had drawn the line in Korea, and he meant it. It was in pursuit of this basic containment policy that Acheson, by then Secretary of State, urged Truman to commit military forces to save South Korea in June 1950.

When the Korean War erupted, American policy changed once again. Had the United States simply sought to contain the Communist thrust into South Korea, it would have restored the 38th parallel, the dividing line between North and South, when it crushed the North Korean army. Instead, American forces under General Douglas MacArthur marched into North Korea and sought to destroy the northern regime and unify the peninsula under President Syngman Rhee. Again, declassified documenta-

UPI/Bettmann Archive

A soldier stands guard on a hill overlooking the demilitarized zone which separates the two Koreas.

tion now shows that this action reflected a change from containment to a new policy, rollback. As policy planners described it, the United States for the first time had the chance to displace and transform some Communist real estate. This American thrust, however, brought Chinese forces in on the northern side; these "volunteers" and a reinvigorated North Korean army pushed U.S. and South Korean forces out of North Korea within a month and caused a crisis in American domestic politics as backers of Truman fought with backers of MacArthur over the Administration's unwillingness to carry the war to mainland China. Although the war lasted another two years, until the summer of 1953, the outcome of early 1951 was definitive: a stalemate, and an American commitment to containment that accepted the de facto reality of two Koreas. That explains why U.S. troops remain in South Korea today.

Soviet Policy

From the time of the czars, Korea has been a concern of Russian security; the Russo-Japanese War of 1905 was fought in part over the disposition of the Korean peninsula. It has often been thought that the Russians saw Korea as a gateway to the Pacific, and especially to warmwater ports. Furthermore, Korea had one of Asia's oldest Communist movements. Thus it would seem that postwar Korea was of great concern to the Soviet Union and that its policy was a simple matter of Sovietizing northern Korea, setting up a puppet state, and then directing it to unify Korea by force in 1950.

Unlike the Americans, the Soviets have no intention of opening top secret archives, and so one cannot be sure of Soviet goals in Korea. One can only deal with the known facts and then make inferences, and even the facts are in dispute. First, the Soviets did not get a warmwater port out of their involvement in Korea. Second, they did not have an effective relationship with the Korean Communists. Soviet dictator Joseph Stalin purged and even shot many of the Koreans who had functioned in the Communist International; he did not help Kim Il Sung and other guerrillas in their struggle against the Japanese. Third, the Soviets let the Koreans twist slowly in the wind during MacArthur's march north in 1950; it was the Chinese who bailed Kim out. And finally, North Korea was not simply a Sovietized puppet state.

One can infer changes in Soviet policy by looking at turning points in 1946 and 1949. During World War II Stalin was mostly silent in discussions with Roosevelt about Korea, tending either to humor FDR and his pet trusteeship projects (which Stalin no doubt thought were naive), or to say that the Koreans would want independence. From 1941 to 1945 Kim Il Sung and other guerrillas were given sanctuary in Sino-Russian border towns near Khabarovsk, trained at a small school, and dispatched as agents into Japanese-held territory. Although the State Department suspected that as many as 30,000 Koreans were being trained as Soviet guerrilla agents, postwar North Korean documents, captured by MacArthur, reveal that these numbers could not have been more than a few hundred. When the Soviets occupied Korea north of the 38th parallel in August 1945, they brought these Koreans (often termed Soviet-Koreans, even though most of them were not Soviet citizens) with them. Kim Il Sung did not appear in North Korea until October 1945, however, and what he did in the two months after the Japanese surrender is not known.

Although the Soviets presented Kim to the Korean people as a guerrilla hero, this was little different from the return of Syngman Rhee in South Korea. From August 1945 until January 1946, the Soviets worked with a coalition of Communists and nationalists, led by a Christian educator named Cho Man-sik. They did not set up a central administration, nor did they create an army. They pursued diplomatic negotiations with the United States on trusteeship (at the Moscow meetings in December 1945). In retrospect their policy seems more tentative and reactive than American policy in South Korea; Soviet power at that time in the Far East was flexible and resulted in the withdrawal of Soviet forces from Manchuria in early 1946. A Soviet Union utterly devastated by the war seemed much more concerned with Eastern Europe.

In 1946 this changed. In February an Interim People's Committee led by Kim Il Sung became the first central government in North Korea; in March in a revolutionary land reform, landlords were dispossessed without compensation; in August a powerful political party (called the North Korean Workers' party) came to dominate politics; and in the fall the first rudiments of a northern army appeared. Powerful central agencies nationalized major industries (they had of course mostly been owned by the Japanese) and began a two-year economic program on the Soviet model, with priority given to heavy industry. Nationalists and Christian leaders were denied all but pro forma participation in politics, and Cho Man-sik was held under house arrest. Kim Il Sung and his allies dominated the press, eliminating newspapers that contained opposition sentiments.

It was in the period 1946–48 that Soviet domination of North Korea was at its height. The Soviets, in particular, sought to involve North Korea in a quasi-colonial relationship in which Korean raw materials such as tungsten and gold were exchanged for Soviet manufactures. Most interestingly, they appear to have sought to keep Chinese Communist influence out of Korea: in the late 1940s Chinese ideology (meaning Maoism or the ideology of Mao Zedong) had to be infiltrated into Korean newspapers and books. The Soviets did not sponsor docile puppets. The Korean guerrillas who fought in Manchuria were not easily molded and dominated. They were tough as nails, highly nationalistic, and determined to have Korea for themselves.

At the end of 1948 the Soviets withdrew their occupation forces from North Korea. This decision contrasted strongly with Soviet policies in Eastern Europe, where in several countries such as East Germany Soviet divisions remain to this day. But no Soviet troops were again stationed in Korea. At the same time, tens of thousands of Korean soldiers who had fought in the Chinese civil war filtered back to Korea. This little known but terribly important episode signaled the beginning of the end of Soviet dominance; all through 1949 tough, crack troops with Chinese, not Soviet, experience returned to be integrated with the Korean People's Army (KPA, formally established in February 1948). Stalin was a consummate realist who had once asked how many divisions the pope could deploy; he would be forced to recognize that the return of these Korean troops would inevitably make North Korea lean toward China. At a minimum they enhanced Kim Il Sung's bargaining power and enabled him to maneuver between the two Communist giants; he has done it ever since.

The Soviets kept advisers in the Korean government and military, continued to trade and to ship weaponry to North Korea. Perhaps they hoped to dominate both North Korea and China and establish a monolithic transnational Communist unit in Northeast Asia. But without military forces, and facing tough customers like Mao and Kim, they could not do so. One may therefore see 1949 as a watershed in Soviet policy, the time when North Korea got some room for maneuver, and when the Soviets sought to distance themselves from the perceived volatility of Kim and his allies.

Although sufficient documentation does not exist to prove the point, it appears now that the Soviets did not order Kim to attack South Korea; if they did have a role in the events of June 1950, it more likely was an attempt to draw American power into a bloody and useless war, and to pit China against the United States and thereby assure China's orientation toward the socialist bloc. In any case when Kim's regime was nearly extinguished in the fall of 1950, the Soviets did very little to save it. China picked up the pieces, and the North Koreans have never forgotten it. From this moment on, North Korea treasured its relationship with China, whereas it dealt with the Soviet Union because it had to.

Building Two States in One Country

The greatest mistake one can make in evaluating postwar Korea is to assume that Koreans were clay to be molded and manipulated by the United States and the Soviet Union. Yet in much of the literature the focus is on big-power actions, and Korea is like an empty "black box" within which Koreans get things done to them. Had there been no Soviet or American occupation, the effects of the colonial period would nonetheless have assured deep divisions within Korean society. The big powers did not introduce communism and capitalism; Koreans had begun discovering both in the 1920s, if not earlier. The big powers could not press buttons and get their way; Koreans proved recalcitrant even to violent pressures. This pattern was apparent in the emergence of separate regimes.

The big powers choose to recognize 1948 as the year in which separate regimes emerged—but that is only because the United States and the Soviet Union take credit for the establishment of the ROK and the DPRK. Actually, both regimes were in place, de facto, by the end of 1946. They each had bureaucratic, police, military, and effective political power. They each had preempted, or at least shaped, the Korea policies of the powers.

In the south, the actual planning for a separate regime began in the last months of 1945. Syngman Rhee, a 70-year-old patriot who had lived in the United States since 1911 (when he earned a Ph.D. at Princeton), returned in October with the backing of

In 1948, at age 73, Dr. Syngman Rhee became president of the Republic of Korea.

UPI/Bettmann Archive

General MacArthur and elements in military and intelligence circles in the United States. A crusty and conservative man of the older generation, he was also a master politician. Within weeks he had won control of conservative and traditionalist factions, many of them from the landed class; he also had found friends amongst Americans worried about the spread of radicalism, who needed little convincing that Rhee and his allies would be a bulwark against communism. In short order, and despite State Department objections, the American occupation forces and Rhee began to make plans for a separate administration of southern Korea, for a southern army (which began training in January 1946), for the reestablishment of a national police force, and for a "Koreanization" of the governmental bureaucracy left by the

Japanese (which was substantially completed by the end of 1946). The Americans staffed the military, the police, and the bureaucracy—except for a few senior officials—with Koreans who had had experience in the colonial regime; they thought they had no other choice, but in so doing the regime took on a reactionary cast that severely weakened it in its competition with the north.

The Americans immediately ran into monumental opposition to such policies from the mass of South Koreans, leading to a sorry mess of strikes, violence, a massive rebellion in four provinces in the fall of 1946, and a significant guerrilla movement in 1948 and 1949. Much of this owed to the unresolved land problem, as conservative land elements used their bureaucratic power to block redistribution of land to tenants. The North Koreans, of course, sought to take advantage of this discontent, but the best evidence shows that most of the dissidents and guerrillas were southerners, upset about southern policies. Indeed, the strength of the left wing was in those provinces most removed from the 38th parallel, in the southwest and the southeast.

By 1947 American authorities came to understand that Syngman Rhee might hurt their cause more than help it; the commander of the occupation, General John R. Hodge, came to distrust and even detest Rhee. Their battles were reminiscent of those between General "Vinegar Joe" Stilwell and Nationalist leader Chiang Kai-shek in China. Still, Rhee knew well that his great "hole card" was the wavering unreliability of more moderate politicians: they might prefer a unified Korea under Kim Il Sung to a separate South Korea under Syngman Rhee. He parlayed this hole card into an American commitment to back the ROK in world forums, even to the point of getting the UN to bless his regime by observing an election and by de facto recognition.

American power was so great that it was able to influence the formal rules of the game of South Korean politics, and thus the 1948 constitution was a relatively liberal document, guaranteeing basic freedoms of speech and press, a vociferous legislature, and periodic elections. It had certain critical loopholes as well, allowing Rhee to proclaim emergencies or use draconian national security laws to deal with his opposition. No one could call South

Korea a liberal democracy before the Korean War, although many Americans hoped that it was at least moving in that direction. There was an extraordinary number of political executions, and thousands of political prisoners were held in Rhee's jails. Korea's intrepid journalists, however, did periodically blast the regime in a press freer than that of South Korea today and of North Korea in any period since 1945.

The Rhee regime also wanted to unify Korea under its rule, by force if necessary. Rhee often referred to a "northern expedition" to "recover the lost territory," and in the summer of 1949 his army provoked the majority of the fighting along the 38th parallel (according to formerly secret American documents), fighting that sometimes took hundreds of lives. This was a prime reason why the United States refused to supply tanks and airplanes to the ROK: it feared that they would be used to attack North Korea. When Acheson delivered his famous speech in January 1950, in which he appeared to place South Korea outside the American defense perimeter in Asia, he was mainly seeking to remind Rhee that he could not count on automatic American backing, regardless of how he behaved.

The North Korean regime emerged de facto in 1946, and looked forward to a military expedition—to the south. Within a year of liberation North Korea had a powerful political party, a budding army, and the mixed blessing of a single leader named Kim Il Sung. By mid-1946 he had placed close, loyal allies at the heart of power. His prime assets were his background, his skills at organization, and his ideology.

Although Kim was 34 when he came to power, few other Koreans who were still alive could match his record of resistance to the Japanese. He was fortunate to emerge in the last decade of a 40-year resistance that had killed off many leaders of the older generation. The DPRK today absurdly claims that Kim was the leader of all Korean resisters, when in fact there were many. But he was able to win the support and firm loyalty of several hundred people like him: young, tough, nationalistic guerrillas who had fought in Manchuria. The prime test of legitimacy in postwar Korea was one's record under the hated Japanese regime, and so Kim and his core allies possessed nationalist credentials that were superior to those of the Rhee leadership. Furthermore, Kim's backers had military force at their disposal and used it to advantage against rivals with no military experience.

Kim's organizational skills probably came from his experience in the Chinese Communist party in the 1930s. Unlike traditional Korean leaders—and many more intellectual or theoretical Communists—he pursued a style of mass leadership, using his considerable charisma, the practice of going down to the factory or the farm for "on-the-spot guidance," and encouraging his allies always to do the same. The North Koreans went against Soviet orthodoxy by including masses of poor peasants in the Korean Workers' party (KWP), and indeed terming it a mass rather than a vanguard party. Since the 1940s the DPRK has enrolled 12 to 14 percent of the population in the Korean Workers' party, compared to 1 to 3 percent for most Communist parties. Data from captured documents show that the vast majority of party members had been peasants with no previous political experience. Membership in the party gave them position, prestige, privileges, and a rudimentary form of political participation.

From the beginning of 1946, Kim's ideology tended to be revolutionary-nationalist rather than Communist. He talked about Korea, not about the Communist International. He spoke of unification, not national division. He discussed nationalism, not Marxism. He distributed land to the tillers instead of collectivizing it (at least until the Korean War began). One can also see in the late 1940s the beginnings of the Juche ideology so ubiquitous in North Korea today, a doctrine stressing self-reliance and independence.

Kim's great political weapon was his control of the party and the army. He systematically filtered his allies through the commanding heights of each; when the KPA was founded in 1948 it was said to have grown out of Kim's guerrilla army and to have inherited its "revolutionary tradition." When masses of Koreans who had fought with the Chinese Communists came back to Korea in 1949, and thereby threatened Kim's power, he had

37

himself declared *suryong* or "supreme leader," a designation that had only been used for Stalin until that time.

Although there remain many murky aspects of the Korean War, it now seems that the frontal attack in June 1950 was mainly Kim's decision, and that the key enabling factor was the presence of as many as 100,000 troops with battle experience in China. When the Rhee regime, with American military advisers, largely eliminated the guerrilla threat in the winter of 1949–50, the civil war moved into a conventional phase. Had the Americans stayed out, the northern regime would have won easily; as it happened, however, Kim's regime was nearly extinguished. When the war finally ended, the North had been devastated by three years of bombing attacks that hardly left a modern building standing. Both Koreas had watched as a virtual holocaust ravaged their country and turned the vibrant expectations of 1945 into a nightmare.

The point to remember, perhaps, is that it was a civil war and, as a British diplomat once said, "every country has a right to have its 'War of the Roses.'" The true tragedy was not the war itself, for a civil conflict purely amongst Koreans might have resolved the extraordinary tensions generated by colonialism and national division. The tragedy was that the war solved nothing: only the status quo ante was restored. Today the tensions and the problems remain.

4

The South Korean
Political System

The post-Korean War era has been marked by relative political stability interrupted by periodic crises, making it difficult to characterize the period as a whole. South Korea has been more stable than many developing nations, which may suffer coups every six months. Yet there have been coups. It has had but three important leaders; however, there is as yet no experience of stable transition to a new leader. It has had long periods of politics as usual, but giving way to devastating disorders. The best explanation for this pattern is probably the tensions generated by very rapid change.

The ROK economy has gone from stagnant poverty to dynamic growth and considerable wealth in one generation; this is the most important single change (see Chapter 6). New political forces have emerged, the most important being the military and burgeoning middle and working classes. New institutions, from the corporate conglomerates to the Korean Central Intelligence Agency (KCIA), have transformed the political economy and the role of the state. The political system itself has changed dramatically. And new tensions have arisen in an older relationship, that between the United States and Korea.

Student Revolution and the Opposition Regime

The aged Syngman Rhee continued to rule in South Korea until 1960. He presided over a dismal situation of war-torn devastation, reconstruction and rehabilitation, and relative economic stagnation. The Korean War did eliminate some recalcitrant problems, if violently. The paradoxical effect of the three-month North Korean occupation of the South in 1950 (coupled with behind-the-scenes American pressure) was to make possible land reform and the end of landlord dominance in the countryside. Many landlords had been eliminated, or had fled, or had come to believe that they could not restore their influence. Thus the age-old balance between the central state and rural power was definitely transformed, and the state benefited. Also, the war effectively ended the strong threat from the left. Radical peasant and labor organizations, as well as the formerly strong guerrillas, largely disappeared by the mid-1950s. The left's influence remained as an important residual or subliminal force, but it lacked organization and expression. This led the way to a diffuse authoritarianism in the period 1953–60, one that allowed a limited pluralism and a moderately free press; there was no space for leftists or independent labor unions, but perhaps more than before for intellectuals, students, and the moderate opposition.

What remained unchanged was the fundamental character of the Rhee regime: its police and military holdovers from the colonial period, its authoritarian bent, its use of the state to preserve power rather than to stimulate the economy. Americans, in particular, were upset by the inability of Rhee and his allies to get the economy going and growing; furthermore, the United States had by the end of the war an immense military, political, and administrative presence in Korea (military bases, a large embassy, a big economic assistance mission) and provided about five sixths of the ROK's imports in direct grants and subsidies. It did not want this investment wasted, and therefore helped prepare the ground for a new, dynamic economic program.

In 1960, large student protests triggered by an election scandal toppled the 85-year-old Rhee, during what is known as the April Revolution. Rhee retired to Hawaii, where he died in 1965, and the opposition came to power. In many ways Korea's modern students have inherited the Confucian dictum that scholars should be activists in politics and moral examples to others. Thus 1960 was one of their finest hours, and since that time they often have stood for—and suffered for—democratization and basic human rights. They and the common people who joined them during the April Revolution also made possible the partial completion of the agenda of liberation in 1945: the police and army were purged of many Koreans who had served the Japanese.

The moderate opposition to the Rhee regime organized the Second Republic, which lasted less than a year until replaced by a military coup. The most democratic of Korea's postwar regimes, it was also the weakest. The Democratic party under Chang Myon had a majority, but it was basically the same conservative grouping of yangbans and landed elements that had emerged in 1945. Americans tended to like this group far better than the Rhee group, and Chang Myon was a particular favorite. But the group's liberalism was weak, it tended to oppose a strong executive, and the inordinate influence of American thinking on its members caused other Koreans to question its nationalist credentials. During 1960–61 the Second Republic tolerated boisterous student demonstrations, interference with the parliament, a noisy press, and, as the year wore on, an increasingly radicalized segment that wanted unification talks with the North.

The Park Period, 1961–79

In May 1961 a new element stepped into Korean politics, a modern military organization of younger officers, most trained in the post-1945 period. Members of the second and eighth classes of the Korean Military Academy, graduated in 1946 and 1949 respectively, mounted a bloodless coup that put an end to the Chang regime. South Korea has not got free of this military influence yet: a retired general still runs the government, and retired generals are prominent in most major institutions—the corporations, the National Assembly, much of political life as a whole. The leader of the 1961 coup was General Park Chung Hee, trained first by the Japanese and then by the United States, active in military intelligence during the Korean War, and, like many other officers of his generation, upset with the privileges, the corruption, and the incompetence of senior military officials during the Rhee period. He ruled until 1963 on a classic junta pattern, vowing to rid Korea of corruption and get the economy moving.

Park donned civilian clothes and ran for election in 1963 under intense pressure from the Kennedy Administration to redress the rampant human rights violations. He won that election, and another in 1967, and another in 1971. The 1963 election was perhaps the freest in postwar Korea, and it coincided with a new constitution, written with private American help, that sought to disperse and confine executive power in a stronger legislature and a two-party system that would legitimate strong opposition. But as with the Chang Myon regime, this reflected American preferences and was an index of South Korea's dependency upon the United States. It was not Park's preferred political system, and it harmed his nationalist image.

Park's preferences were better represented in two new institutions that emerged in the 1960s, the Democratic Republican party (DRP) and the KCIA. The former was really the first effective political party in postwar Korea; it was modeled less on American parties than on the quasi-Leninist Kuomintang (or Nationalist party) of pre-Communist China, having a democratic-centralist internal structure, a permanent secretariat, and funding from the regime and private supporters. A critical problem of rapid development is to dovetail economic growth with an organization capable of channeling and containing newly mobilized forces in the interests of stability. The DRP intended to be such an organization. It was also a personal political machine for Park, although its founder and an ally in the coup, Kim Jong-pil, soon came to rival Park for power.

Kim also was the organizer of the KCIA (with American CIA help), an agency that combined the functions of our CIA and FBI, and broadened those activities as years went by. From the inception every KCIA director has been a potential rival for presidential power, and in 1979 its director put an end to the Park regime by shooting Park to death over dinner one October night.

Students at Korea University in Seoul hurl rocks at riot police in one of a series of clashes in spring 1971.

Nonetheless, until the 1970s its role was relatively limited; only after the political system itself changed did the KCIA become a dominant institution in Korean political life.

A new, formally authoritarian political system had emerged in 1971–72, known as the Yushin system. By the end of 1972, the National Assembly had become a creature of executive power—a rubber stamp; indirect presidential elections replaced the direct vote and made Park in effect president-for-life; the regime muzzled the press and much intellectual dissent by stationing KCIA officers and censors in newspaper offices and universities; the opposition parties were systematically surveilled and harassed, leading to the kidnapping of Kim Dae-jung in Tokyo in August 1973; finally dissenters were subjected to tortures that made South Korea a prime target of Amnesty International, and a prime problem for American policy. In addition, the KCIA began operating fairly openly in the United States and other countries, intimidating Korean communities abroad and even attempting to bribe congressmen. The latter effort extended beyond Congress to business and academic circles; when this large influence-buying effort became public in the course of congressional and Justice Department investigations, it got the title Koreagate and deeply affected Korean-American relations in the mid-1970s.

What were the reasons for this qualitative change in Korean politics, away from at least formal democratic procedure, toward substantive and frank authoritarianism? The obvious explanation is the threat to Park's rule posed by the 1971 election. Kim Dae-jung, a young charismatic leader from the southwestern provinces, had breathed life into the opposition, and unlike previous opposition candidates, he could not be linked to the hated colonial period, or to the 1940s' struggles to preserve landed power. He got 46 percent of the vote, in spite of widespread regime attempts to manipulate the election, buy votes, and mobilize supporters at the polls. There were deeper reasons as well. Park himself cited the changing international environment as his justification for Yushin, and indeed 1971–72 did bring big changes. The Nixon Administration opened relations with China, North Korea's ally, began to withdraw a division of American troops from South Korea, and bargained hard on Korean textile exports to the U.S. market. For the first time since 1953, the ROK could not count on automatic American backing: the cold war was ending around Korea, if not in Korea. This was a key reason for Koreagate: in the adverse climate created by the Vietnam war, the Park regime sought to build congressional support for a favorable U.S. policy toward Korea.

Nineteen hundred seventy-one was also the first year of relative economic downturn since the ROK's export-led program took off in the mid-1960s. Furthermore, the Third Five-Year Plan, 1971–76, inaugurated a phase of heavy industrialization: new steel, petrochemical, auto, shipbuilding and nuclear industries were part of this audacious program, devised by economic nationalists who resented Korea's dependence on outside sources for heavy industrial materials. American planners resisted these developments, arguing that Korea's small domestic market would lead to problems of surplus and idle capacity. Park, however, clearly sided with the economic nationalists. In a pithy 1972 slogan he declared that "steel equals national power," and laced his rhetoric with calls for self-reliance and for "Korean-style" politics.

Although all of these factors played a part in the emergence of the Yushin system, the most important was the deepening industrialization program. In the 1970s Korea bore close comparison to so-called bureaucratic-authoritarian regimes that proliferated in Latin America and that, as in the case of Argentina, linked a strong state to a heavy industrialization program, nationalism and neo-mercantilism, and a repressive deactivation of groups opposed to this course, such as labor unions and small businesses. The great problem in Korea was that labor had never really been activated in the first place and the urban working and middle classes were growing rapidly and yet finding less space for political representation than in the 1960s. Finally, a daunting paradox of Yushin was that the ROK became more authoritarian as its economy became more successful, exactly the reverse of what American liberals had hoped for. South Korea was more democratic when it had a per capita income of $200 in 1960 than it was with a per capita income of $800 in 1978.

The Crisis of 1979–80 and the Rise of Chun Doo Hwan

In the spring of 1979, with economic problems again mounting with the "second oil shock," and no relaxation of political restrictions, a crisis erupted that destroyed the Park regime. It began with markedly enhanced opposition power deployed around Kim Dae-jung, who drew support from textile workers, small businesses and firms with national rather than international interests, students and intellectuals, and his native southwestern region which had historically been rebellious and which had been untouched by much of the growth of the previous 15 years. (Park was from the southeast and had poured all sorts of investment into that region.) In August 1979 Kim's opposition party joined striking textile workers, a woman died in a police melee, and shortly thereafter major urban insurrections occurred in Pusan and Masan. Unlike previous demonstrations, these included workers and commoners and fed upon grievances of unemployed or underemployed urban workers.

In circumstances that remain mysterious, but appear to be related to dissatisfaction with the way Park was handling all the dissent, Kim Jae Kyu, KCIA director, shot Park to death on the night of October 26, and then was himself arrested in what seemed to have been a bungled coup attempt. Nonetheless, the regime collapsed and thereby demonstrated how much ROK politics still depended on firm control by a single leader. In the months that followed, there were hopeful developments, and ominous ones.

During the first months of 1980 Korean citizens participated widely and effectively in meetings around the country about a new constitution, about political parties and election rules, really about what sort of democratic system ought to replace Yushin. But in December 1979, a young officer, Chun Doo Hwan, had seized effective power within the military in a coup in which several high officers were killed. Chun had been a protégé of Park Chung Hee, had commanded Korean troops in the Vietnam war, and was head of the powerful Defense Security Command at the time of the assassination.

During March and April 1980 students were quite active but they confined their demonstrations to Seoul's campuses. In late April, however, miners seized a small town and held it for a week, and Chun had himself declared head of the KCIA. Thereafter, students and commoners poured into the streets. In mid-May hundreds of thousands of protesters filled Seoul in demonstrations unprecedented since 1960. Martial law was declared, which in turn touched off a rebellion in the southwest, centered in the provincial capital of Kwangju. Rebels held the city and some surrounding towns for a week. Chun and his allies put down the rebellion with great brutality and loss of life: official figures say 300 civilians died, but dissidents believe the figure to be over 1,000. Chun then went on to become president of the ROK and to establish a Fifth Republic, but he remains tainted by his role in the bloodletting in Kwangju.

Seoul, Nov. 3, 1979: The funeral procession of President Park Chung Hee en route to Seoul's capital building.

The Kwangju rebellion was the worst political crisis in the ROK since the Korean War. For a time it seemed that South Korea might disintegrate as did Iran in 1979, but in contrast to Iran the military did not fracture internally and the rebellion remained primarily regional rather than national. Nonetheless it remains a deep wound in the body politic, and a sign of a much deeper level of dissatisfaction than most observers would have expected.

The Chun government has not suffered a repetition of such serious disorder, and on the surface politics has returned to the pattern of stability marked by minor demonstrations and strikes. Some 15,000 arrested protesters were given a type of "reeducation" after Kwangju, and about 800 politicians from the Park era were proscribed from political participation. Chun and his allies brought Kim Dae-jung up on sedition charges and convicted him, saying he was responsible for Kwangju. Most observers think that only U.S. intervention saved Kim from being executed.

In the early 1980s a new political elite emerged, along with wholly new political parties. Several amnesties have released political prisoners, and the number of politicians proscribed from activity is down to 250—but this includes all the older, most important ones. There are few trees still standing amid Seoul's previous political forest. Chun has abolished some of the more absurd manifestations of authoritarianism, such as the nightly curfew that had been in effect since 1945, and the Japanese-military-style uniforms that all schoolboys used to wear. But the political system remains fundamentally Park's Yushin system under new guise.

In October 1983 a bomb blast in Rangoon, Burma, decimated Chun's Cabinet and very nearly killed Chun himself. A Burmese court determined that North Korean terrorists had carried out this despicable act, and Burma proceeded to break diplomatic relations with Pyongyang. The blast also took with it a number of pro-Western, moderate officials who had been urging Chun to loosen political restraints. Assuming that this was a North Korean act (the evidence introduced at the trial was sketchy and incomplete), the North Koreans presumably acted on the assumption that killing Chun would have an effect similar to the Park assassination of 1979: the removal of the maximum leader inflicts chaos on the political system. Unfortunately, they are probably right, and this underscores the continuing tenuousness of the South Korean system.

There are some constants in South Korean politics in the period 1961–84 that should be noted. First, the military remains the most powerful single grouping, followed by the intelligence bureaucracy. Second, the military itself is divided into age and regional groupings. Groups cohere around particular officer classes: the second and the eighth in the Park period, and the 1955 military academy class in the Chun period. Civilian political groups also divide regionally, and in both the Park and the Chun periods the southeastern Kyongsang provinces have been vastly overrepresented both in the leadership and in the state and corporate sector. (This was an important reason for the southwestern rebellion in 1980.) Third, a profound hostility continues to

UPI/Bettmann Archive

General Chun Doo Hwan (shown above with his wife in August 1980) retired from the army shortly before assuming the presidency of the ROK.

exist between military officers who are primarily of non-yangban peasant stock, and students, intellectuals, and much of the opposition party.

The political system still does not have viable political parties. Although the ruling party is always the strongest by virtue of its government support, internal structure and superior funding, it has not replaced the military itself or the intelligence structure as a core element of stable politics. Opposition parties tend to continue the old pattern of patron-client ties, in which factions cluster around a single leader. Voting is of little importance and the pattern remains what some scholars have called mobilized voting, that is, people go to the polls because they are ordered to, or think they should as a duty to the ruler, or because they are paid to go, but not because they have much sense of participation. Finally, the system has not escaped a single-leader principle, nor has it managed a successful leadership transition; both mean that when the maximum leader dies or is killed, chaos may ensue.

5

The North Korean
Political System

The DPRK has a political system that is not easy to understand, to state the case mildly. It is among the world's most
closed, impenetrable regimes, with a totally controlled press,
sharp restrictions on travel in and out of the country, no "listening
points" where defectors collect (like Hong Kong for China), and
an ideology of self-reliance that often matches the "exclusionism"
of the traditional period.

Yet there is one fascinating window on the DPRK, provided by
a large collection of documents captured during the Korean War
and now available to scholars. Also in the past decade the regime
has allowed most of the Americans who specialize in Korean
studies to make short visits for a few weeks of carefully controlled
observation (this writer included). These windows, combined
with frequent and careful reading of the press, can make possible
some generalizations.

The first generalization is that because of the extraordinary
longevity and relative stability of the regime, its origins in the
1940s can still tell us much about today. The maximum leader,
Kim Il Sung, came into effective power in early 1946 and still

rules in 1984. Now 72, he has all along surrounded himself with comrades connected to the guerrilla struggle against Japan. In the 1940s he faced factional power struggles between his Manchurian group, Communists who had remained in Korea during the colonial period (the "domestic" faction), Koreans associated with Chinese communism (termed the "Yenan faction"), and Koreans from or close to the U.S.S.R. (the "Soviet faction"). In the aftermath of the Korean War, amid much false scapegoating for the disasters of the war, Kim purged the domestic faction, many of whose leaders were from southern Korea. In the mid-1950s he eliminated key leaders of the Soviet faction and overcame an apparent coup attempt by members of the Yenan faction. None of these power struggles was as destabilizing as, say, the Stalin-Trotsky feud in Russia or the Cultural Revolution in China; what is more striking, they ensued during only the first decade of the regime and have not been repeated in the past quarter century. There have been conflicts within the leadership, but they have been relatively minor and have not successfully challenged Kim's power.

The DPRK, like the People's Republic of China, originated in a period of maximum Soviet influence and therefore has the typical structure associated with all Soviet-linked Marxist-Leninist regimes: a strong, highly organized vanguard party; centralized, top-down administration by weighty bureaucracies; an economy in which goods and services are allocated according to central, long-term plans rather than market principles; collectivized agriculture and relative priority to heavy industry over light; and an ideology traced to Marx and Lenin which places the DPRK in the stage of "building socialism" toward a distant final phase of communism. But there is much more to the political system than just this.

A China Model?

Marxism presented no political model for achieving socialism, only an opaque set of prescriptions. This political vacuum opens the way to an assertion of indigenous political culture and may even demand it by virtue of the very paucity of political models.

The DPRK leadership was probably most deeply influenced by the Chinese Communist model, and so Kim is very much a "mass line" leader like Mao, making frequent visits to factories and the countryside, sending cadres "down" to local levels to help policy implementation and to solicit local opinion, requiring small-group political study and so-called criticism and self-criticism, using periodic campaigns to mobilize people for production or education, and encouraging soldiers to engage in production in good "people's army" fashion. The DPRK, like China but unlike the U.S.S.R., maintains a "united front" policy toward non-Communist groups, so that in addition to the ruling Korean Workers' party there are much smaller parties that have mainly symbolic functions.

North Korean Divergences

There are many differences from China and the U.S.S.R., however, and many of them have been there since the founding of the DPRK. The symbol of the KWP, for example, is a hammer and sickle with a writing brush superimposed, symbolizing the "three-class alliance" of workers, peasants and intellectuals. Unlike Mao's China, the Kim regime has never excoriated intellectuals as a potential "new class" of exploiters; instead it has followed an inclusive policy toward them, perhaps because postwar Korea was so short of intellectuals and experts, and because so many left the north for the south in the 1945–50 period. The term intellectual refers to experts and technocrats, not dissenters and critics, of which there must be exceedingly few in North Korea, even when compared to China and the Soviet Union. The relatively sophisticated industrial structure that the DPRK began with in 1945 required a higher proportion of experts and created labor shortages in agriculture, thereby stimulating mechanization of farming. This also is quite different from China.

In contrast to the typical Marxist-Leninist model, the Korean Workers' party is less a tiny vanguard than a big "mass party," as mentioned earlier, which then raises the question, what is the vanguard? It is what Kim calls the core or nucleus at the

President Kim Il Sung (center) addresses the sixth congress of the Korean Workers' party in Pyongyang in 1980. The banner carries his portrait and KWP symbol, a hammer, sickle, and writing brush, representing the alliance of workers, peasants and intellectuals.

commanding heights of the regime, consisting of himself and his closest associates; all "good things" emanate in top-down fashion from this core, in sharp departure from Chinese dicta about the source of good ideas being the mass of peasants and workers. But this principle of core leadership is just the beginning of the DPRK's unique political system, and it is here that indigenous Korean political culture is most pronounced.

North Korean Corporatism and the Juche Idea

The term that perhaps best captures this system is socialist corporatism—the organization of a society into industrial and professional corporations for political purposes. Although corporatism is historically associated with conservative, even fascist regimes, there has been since the 1920s a particular strain of leftist corporatist thinking which argues that nation-state conflict has replaced class conflict as the motive force of history. North Korea was the first example of postcolonial socialism; the colonial heritage of dependency and underdevelopment has deeply affected North Korean politics.

If nation-state conflict is the point, then one would emphasize masses rather than classes, that is, national unity rather than workers fighting bourgeois intellectuals; one would have a mass party, not a class party of proletarians. North Korean ideology calls for absolute unity at home, and self-reliance and independence vis-à-vis the rest of the world. One cannot open a DPRK newspaper or listen to a single speech without hearing about Juche. The North Koreans fund and organize Juche study groups all over the world. The term was first used in a 1955 speech where Kim castigated some of his comrades for being too pro-Soviet—thinking that if the Soviets eat fish on Monday, Koreans should too, etc. But it really means placing all foreigners at arm's length, and resonates deeply with Korea's Hermit Kingdom past.

Juche has no meaning for a Marxist, but much for East Asians. It shares a Chinese character with the *t'i-yung* phrase popular in late-19th century China and with the Japanese *kokutai* of the 1930s. T'i-yung meant Chinese learning as the basis, Western learning or technology for its utility. Kokutai was a somewhat mystical term meant to distinguish all that was uniquely Japanese from all that was alien and foreign. Juche takes Korean ideas as basic, foreign ideas as secondary; it also suggests putting Korean things first at all times. By the 1970s Juche had triumphed fundamentally over Marxism-Leninism as the basic ideology of the regime, but the emphases had been there from its beginning.

North Korea's goal of tight unity at home has produced a remarkably organic politics in the recent past, unprecedented in any existing Communist regime. Kim is not just the "iron-willed, ever-victorious commander," the "respected and beloved Leader"; he is also the "head and heart" of the body politic (once, "the supreme brain of the nation"!). The flavor of this politics can only be gotten through quotation (from party newspapers in the spring of 1981):

> Kim Il Sung ... is the great father of our people. .... Long is the history of the word father being used as a word representing love and reverence ... expressing the unbreakable blood ties between the people and the leader. Father. This familiar word represents our people's single heart of boundless respect and loyalty. .... The love shown by the Great Leader for our people is the love of kinship. Our respected and beloved Leader is the tender-hearted father of all the people. .... Love of paternity ... is the noblest ideological sentiment possessed only by our people. ....
>
>   *   *   *
>
> His heart is a traction power attracting the hearts of all people and a centripetal force uniting them as one. .... Kim Il Sung is the great sun and great man ... thanks to this great heart, national independence is firmly guaranteed.

The party is often referred to as the "Mother" party, the party line is said to provide "blood ties," the leader is always "fatherly," and the country is one big (happy?) "family." Kim is paternal and devoted and benevolent, and the people respond with loyalty and obedience and mutual love. This rhetoric has escalated since Kim's son, Kim Jong Il (now 42 years old) has become the designated successor.

Kim's family is, of course, the model family—including his parents, grandparents, great-grandparents, and numerous other relatives, all of whom were appropriately "revolutionary" and dedicated to Korea's independence. Unlike the Maoists, the regime has never meddled with family affairs of its citizens, and indeed the family is termed the core unit of society in the constitution, and the society is called a "great integrated entity."

DPRK socialism possesses a pronounced voluntarism, something also characteristic of corporate politics. The Korean propagandists say that "everything is decided by idea," directly contradicting the materialism at the heart of Marxism. And, of course, the leader's ideas are the best, compounded by his firm "will," always described as "ironlike," or "steellike." Kim invented Juche, and all Koreans "must have Juche firm in mind and spirit," and only then can they be good "Kimilsungists," and only then can the revolution be successful.

The more one seeks to understand Juche, the more the meaning recedes. It is a state of mind, not an idea, and one that is unavailable to the non-Korean. It is the opaque core of what one could call North Korean national solipsism.

National Solipsism and Concentric Circles

National solipsism is a useful term, for it expresses something one comes across all the time in North Korean writings: an assumption that Korea is the center of the world, something that would not occur to a non-Korean. Korea is the center, radiating outward the rays of Juche, especially to third-world nations who are thought by the North Koreans to be ready for Juche. The world leans toward Korea, with all eyes on Kim Il Sung. This is perhaps the most bizarre aspect of the DPRK, but also one of the most palpable. Its parallel is, of course, the Sinocentrism of the Middle Kingdom, this time writ small. But it also expresses a model of concentric circles that is profoundly Korean and that has characterized the DPRK since 1946.

The North Korean system is not simply a hierarchical structure of party, army and state bureaucracies, but it is also a hierarchy of ever-widening concentric circles—somewhat like the old RCA radio signal as depicted in advertisements. At the center is Kim. The next circle is his family, the next, the guerrillas who fought with him, then come the KWP elite. This forms the core circle, and it controls everything at the commanding heights of the regime. Here politics is primarily personalistic, resting on something akin to oaths of fealty and obligation. The core must constantly be steeled and hardened, while moving outward and downward concentrically to encompass other elements of the population, and to provide the glue holding the system together. In the shielded area comprising the workers and peasants which surrounds the core, trust gives way to bureaucratic control. Nonetheless the family remains as the model for societal organization.

An outer circle marks off that which is Korean from that which is foreign, a reflection of the extraordinary ethnic and linguistic unity of Koreans, and Korea's history of exclusionism. Yet the circle keeps on moving, as if to encompass foreigners under the mantle of Kim and his Juche idea. Kim, his flatterers say, is not only a modern "Sun King" at home (referred to as "the Sun of the Nation") but a beacon to the world as well.

This governmental system is instinctively repellent to anyone who identifies with the modern liberal idea, or indeed with the modern Marxist idea. The DPRK's simple adherence to Juche would be one thing, but by trumpeting such ideas far and wide the DPRK has earned widespread disbelief and ridicule. Nonetheless the Kim regime is different. And the difference can only be explained by reference to the tradition and the political culture from whence it came. It is a mixture of Confucian holdovers, Korean traditionalism, and socialist corporatism.

The strength and stability of the system rest on marrying traditional forms of legitimacy, plus a good measure of repression, to modern bureaucratic structures, with the peculiar charisma of Kim Il Sung providing the transition and the cement between the two. The weakness is that core political power seems still to rest upon personalistic ties, with trust barely extending beyond the leader's family and his long-time guerrilla associates. As in South Korea, this suggests a troubled transition once Kim passes from the scene.

6

The Two Economies

The two Korean economies present great contrasts to each other. One has an export-led system, the other a heavy-industry-led system. One is intermeshed with the world economy, the other seeks self-reliance. One has an open door, the other a closed door. Consumer goods and conspicuous wealth prevail in the South, capital goods and a chaste egalitarianism in the North. Seoul is a modern cosmopolitan city with a bustling, crowded downtown; Pyongyang is a modern city with a rustic, antiquarian atmosphere and a sparse, if busy, population. The ROK has witnessed a rapid economic development known as the "miracle on the Han," whereas the DPRK is lagging far behind and is in debt up to its ears.

On closer inspection, however, some of the differences give way to similarities. Seoul has pushed heavy industry in the past 15 years. Pyongyang has made exports a priority in the 1980s. The North imported an entire panty-hose factory in the early 1970s, just as the South began talking about self-reliance. The model villages and model apartments that both regimes show to foreigners as indexes of modernization turn out to be nearly identical—

even in architecture and taste. In both capital cities elite Koreans have been seen pulling up to a barber shop in a shiny new Mercedes and jumping inside for the latest razor-cut. Both have officials in finely tailored suits, sporting Rolex watches. Both want to show the visitor their latest advanced technology (and in both cases it is usually imported). Both have external debt burdens. Finally, neither side has produced a miracle, but both are among the leading cases of rapid development in the world, if on contrasting models.

Export-Led South Korea

Until the early 1960s South Korea had pursued a typical, but fitful and largely unsuccessful, program to substitute domestic products for imports in such industries as textiles, cement, and plate glass. These were incubated and protected behind walls of tariffs and overvalued exchange rates. People with money to invest found the most profit in using government connections to

A nighttime view of Seoul

Courtesy of Korean National Tourism Corporation

get hold of companies formerly held by the Japanese, often making windfalls. Personal and political connections were more important than enterprising virtues. This phase ended in 1961–62, with little development and a generally stagnant economy that was a major cause of the instability that led to a coup.

After Park Chung Hee's coup in 1961 the economy became a central part of the regime's planning focus, and of its legitimacy. The state would be used to prime the economic pump and success would be used to satisfy national expectations and keep Park in power. By now South Korea could call upon a large cadre of economists and planners, many of whom had been trained in American universities; they shared a basic economic outlook with the Americans in the economic aid mission, the embassy, and institutions like the World Bank. New institutions like the Economic Planning Board (EPB) emerged to guide long-term plans (the first since the colonial period) for economic development.

With American support (and often pressure) the ROK in the early 1960s revalued its currency downward (making its exports much cheaper), provided state guarantees for businesses seeking foreign loans, gave tax holidays, exemptions, or reductions to firms willing to produce for the export market, and developed plans for pushing export growth ahead at double-digit rates. Within a few years, exporting became a celebrated national pastime and patriotic activity, with Park blessing every new threshold of achievement.

South Korea led from comparative advantage, meaning primarily its relatively educated and diligent workers and their comparatively low pay. American and Japanese firms were encouraged to relocate there, where productivity was high and labor cost low. The typical industries were textiles, light electronic manufactures like radios and calculators, and simple work and assembly processes such as stamping out nuts and bolts or gluing transistor boards. The foreign firms provided the requisite technologies and a far-flung network of existing markets. Since textiles and light electronics were industries in decline in both Japan and the United States, South Korea, with its disciplined labor force, was a good bet to receive these industries and maintain their competitiveness in world markets. The gains for foreign firms were often remarkable. One Korean economist estimated that assembly workers in the Masan "Free Export Zone" were two and a half times as productive as American labor in the same industry, at one tenth the cost, yielding a 25-fold cost savings.

The export-led program took off in the mid-1960s, in the period of the Second Five-Year Plan. According to some estimates the ROK was for the next decade the most productive economy in the world, having an average annual industrial production growth rate of 25 percent and an incremental capital-output ratio (the amount of capital necessary to produce an additional unit of output) of 0.022, lowest in the world. Its per capita GNP increased from $200 in 1960 to $800 by 1978, and the GNP itself went from $6 billion to $25 billion in the 1965–78 period. Exports were the major engine of this growth, increasing by 45 percent per year on the average in the early and mid-1970s.

This remarkable success is generally thought to be attributable to (1) South Korea's heavy investments in human resources, yielding a highly educated stratum of specialists and high rates of literacy and skills in the population as a whole; (2) long-range planning and administrative guidance by skilled technocrats; (3) a relatively high domestic savings rate; (4) an "abundant and unorganized" working class, in economist Paul W. Kuznets' words; (5) a world economy open to light-industrial exports in the decade after 1965, combined with much American and Japanese help in getting the economy moving.

Koreans, like Japanese, tend to work very hard at middle-school and high-school levels, yielding a population that tends to be ahead of high-school graduates in the West in basic skills. The role of the state is similar to that in Japan as well, with the EPB performing a guiding function in the economy. A major recent study of the South Korean economy by a group of Harvard scholars concluded that "Korea, Inc." is a fairer characterization of the ROK's political economy than is Japan's "Japan, Inc." label: the state is chairman of the board, they say, with an even greater role in the economy than in Japan. Of particular importance is the credit function of the government. The regime is the broker for foreign loans, and thus is able to direct capital to productive, dynamic firms producing for export, and to penalize firms that are doing poorly. This capital provisioning function is a key element of the South Korean model of development, for it allows the state to select and foster firms that have comparative advantages in world markets.

Industrial Expansion

As the economy has grown, so has concentration in industry. Huge firms (such as Hyundai, Daewoo, the Lucky group) have emerged, many of which are now amongst the few hundred largest firms in the world. They are sufficiently concentrated so as to resemble the zaibatsu of prewar Japan, and like them they tend to be highly interpenetrated by the founding families. The Harvard study found that about two thirds of the big firms have the original founder or his offspring at the head. Still, the state remains the maker and the breaker of these conglomerates; they cannot afford to antagonize the state executive.

As the economy developed, Park Chung Hee and the more nationalistic of his allies sought to make the system more self-reliant by deepening the industrial base. The Third Five-Year Plan, in particular, was written by economic nationalists and spawned enormous capital investments in such heavy industries as autos, steel, shipbuilding, petrochemicals, and nuclear-power generation. South Korea was able to install the world's most productive integrated steel mill in P'ohang (with the aid of Japanese technology and capital), and quickly began to make inroads in world steel markets. Today the ROK and Brazil are making steel more efficiently than any other countries, and are running into protectionist pressures from American steel manufacturers. As part and parcel of this new program, the Park government invested in major infrastructure improvements: four-lane highways, city subways, seaports and airports, and communications systems that have transformed the face of old Korea.

The darker side of this success is that independent labor unions still have no legitimacy, the rural sector has not progressed rapidly and remains dependent on American grains, big export firms have devastated the smaller firms producing for the national market, and, as mentioned earlier, Park combined the big role for the state in the economy with a strong role in the polity, thinking that stability was necessary above all else, thus devastating Korean democracy. The economy is structurally dependent on foreign capital and on technologies and foreign markets often still held by foreign multinational corporations. The help and attentions of the United States and Japan mitigate the problems of dependency, but also place outer limits on South Korean development.

The Crisis of 1979–82

In 1978 the South Korean economic threat to advanced countries was so palpable that Japanese newspapers spoke warily of "the Korean challenge," and U.S. officials worried that they might be getting "another Japan" in Korea. But the export-led program ran aground, detonating political instability and leading to a 6 percent loss of GNP in 1980. Exports were expected to grow by 16 to 20 percent during 1979–82, but they were either stagnant or grew at 2 to 3 percent rates through the end of 1982. As the economy stagnated, South Korea's foreign debt grew to a total of $42 billion by late 1983 (Morgan Guaranty Trust Co. figures), fourth largest in the world.

The reasons for this crisis lay deep in the structure of South Korea's economic activity and therefore were not easily remedied. Exports met with ever-higher protectionist barriers around the world. Technology transfers did not occur as expected, leaving South Korea mainly with diminishing labor cost advantages. Rapidly rising oil prices devastated an economy that had no oil of its own. The small domestic market could not make up for declining foreign markets, causing auto and steel factories to run at 20 or 30 percent of capacity. Rising exports were needed to pay back foreign loans, and when exports fell the loans grew precipitously. Finally, the rapid growth was not evenly distributed, causing grievances at home, particularly when expectations for ever-greater growth were dashed in 1980.

After a profound shaking-out process in 1979–82, one which scared foreign investors and raised questions about the whole export-led program, the ROK seems in 1984 to be back on track. Unlike many Latin American nations, it has not yet had major problems servicing its foreign debt. Exports began growing again in mid-1983 and topped $23 billion by year's end, a result in part of economic revival in the United States and general stability in oil prices. Overall growth was remarkably good in 1983, about 9.2 percent; per capita GNP reached $1,850. The 1984 economic plan projects a 7.5 percent growth rate and an export increase of almost 15 percent. If these targets are reached, then the economy will have recovered fully from the 1979–82 disasters. There will remain a host of potential structural problems, however, that make it unlikely that the ROK will be able to replicate its rapid growth in the 1965–78 period: a heavy debt burden, a small internal market, rising protectionism, and difficulties in technology transfer.

The North Korean Economy

The DPRK has a socialist command economy with long-run plans (seven to ten years recently) and a bias toward heavy industry. It allows only a sharply limited role for market allocation, mainly in the rural sector where peasants sell produce from small private plots. There is almost no small business. It has also sought a self-reliant, independent national economy. Therefore it would seem to be a typical socialist system on the Stalinist model.

There are departures and successes, however, that suggest significant North Korean innovation on the Stalinist model. The delivery of goods and services is often decentralized to the neighborhood or village level, and several provinces are said to be self-reliant in food and consumer goods. Foreign visitors see no long lines at stores and restaurants, and residents claim that there are none: this would be a sharp improvement on the Soviet and

Chinese economies. The DPRK also has one of the more successful socialist agricultural systems. Relying mostly on cooperative farms corresponding to the old natural villages rather than huge state farms, and using material incentives with little apparent ideological bias against them, the DPRK has pushed agricultural production ahead rapidly. World Health Organization officials who visited in 1980 reported that "miracle" strains of rice were in wide use, and the U.S. CIA reported in a published study in 1978 that grain production has grown more rapidly in North Korea than in South, that living standards in rural areas "have probably improved faster than in the South," and that "North Korean agriculture is quite highly mechanized, fertilizer application is probably among the highest in the world, and irrigation projects are extensive." The DPRK claims to have the highest per hectare rice output in the world; although that claim cannot be proved, experts do not question North Korea's general agricultural success.

North Korea inherited a heavy industrial base from the Japanese era, and after several years of reorienting this base to serve its own rather than Japanese needs, heavy industrial production grew rapidly. In the late 1950s annual average rates were among the highest in the world, in the 25–30 percent range. Industrial growth slowed down in the late 1960s as plant depreciation and technological obsolescence took their toll; transportation bottlenecks and fuel resource problems also appeared. Thus in the early 1970s the DPRK imported new Western and Japanese technologies on a relatively large scale, buying whole plants on a binge basis. When world prices for some of the DPRK's mineral exports fell, the DPRK was unable to pay foreign creditors and defaulted on more than $1 billion in debts. In the 1980s, however, many of the creditors have been satisfied and the economy seems to have returned to double-digit growth rates (the DPRK publishes few statistics, and most of those are percentages of previous production).

The 1978 CIA study estimated that DPRK GNP stood at about $10 billion in 1976, roughly half that of the ROK. Both regimes were thought to have equivalent per capita GNPs in

1976, however, which suggests that North Korea's economy is hardly a basket case. In 1979 Kim Il Sung claimed a per capita income of $1,900, but it is not known if the figure is accurate, or how it was calculated. The CIA and many other observers in the late 1970s expected South Korea to pull away from North Korea in the economic race, but the problems of 1979–82 hurt the ROK.

Observers believe that the DPRK produces more coal, iron ore, nonferrous metals, machine tools, and military hardware than does the ROK. Steel production is probably about equal. North Korea puts out internal combustion engines, locomotives, motor-cycles, and various sorts of machine-building items using its own indigenous technology, in contrast to South Korea, which must still import most of these items. The DPRK has become a significant actor in international arms trafficking, selling machine guns, artillery, light tanks and other items to friendly countries such as Zimbabwe and Iran (North Korea traded weaponry for oil with Iran after 1978, accounting for as much as 40 percent of Iranian arms imports in 1982).

North Korea's claims of nearly complete self-reliance are discounted by foreign observers. The Soviet Union and China provide petroleum and coking coal and compete for influence with aid and technicians. The DPRK has done well in using indigenous coal and hydroelectric resources to minimize oil use; it seems that much of the extensive rail system is now electrified, and the use of automobiles is minimal. The pursuit of self-reliance is, of course, primarily a matter of politics and foreign relations; it often sacrifices efficiencies of scale and comparative advantage.

Until the 1970s the DPRK traded almost wholly with the socialist bloc, but in the past 15 years it has diversified its trading partners to include Japan, Western Europe, and various third-world nations. By the mid-1970s 40 percent of its trade was with non-Communist countries, and within the bloc only half was with the U.S.S.R. Exporting has been a priority for several years, although North Korea in no sense has an export-led economy like South Korea's. The focus on exports is to garner foreign exchange

The first North Korean
economic delegation
visits Tokyo in 1972
in search of trade and
technology.

to import advanced technologies needed for further industrial
growth, and to pay for imported oil.

A Visitor's View

American visitors to the DPRK in the early 1980s tended to
come away impressed by what they saw. Crossing into North
Korea from China makes one think one has left a poor country for
a moderately well-off one. The fields are deep green and every
inch of land is carefully tended; construction projects hum with
around-the-clock shifts; people bustle through the streets to work
at all hours; the cities suggest a clean, sparsely populated, diligent
and efficient system. The country has an isolated, antiquarian,
even bucolic atmosphere, as if one were thrown back to the 1940s;
at the same time it has a few world-class facilities, like the

Pyongyang maternity hospital, which is chock full of the latest West German and Hungarian technology. The mass of the people are well-fed and plainly dressed; the elite drive Volvos and Mercedes and tend to be flashy in showing off foreign consumer items like watches.

North Korea faces its own set of structural problems in the economy. Its ponderous bureaucracy is impenetrable and exasperating to foreign businesses. Its dogged desire for self-reliance has alienated the Soviets and placed many obstacles—including the lack of foreign exchange—in the way of trade with the West. Technological obsolescence means North Korea must import if it hopes to compete with South Korea, but it is nowhere near adopting the new policies necessary to gain access to newer technologies, in great contrast to China. Political rigidity has carried over into economic exchange; North Korea failed where South Korea succeeded in trying to buy big steel mills from Japan, and if South Korea installs another integrated mill (as planned), it will leap ahead of North Korea in steel production. As long as the DPRK maintains its stark hostility toward the United States, it will not get the trade and technology that it claims to want and certainly needs.

On balance, however, the stress should be on the comparative economic successes of both Koreas. Both are models of postcolonial development, if on entirely opposite systems. The economic successes contrast starkly with the wretched politics of both (from a liberal point of view). How to account for this? Perhaps by remembering the stress on education in both systems, strong backing from big-power allies, effective use of state intervention in promoting economic development, and above all by remembering the simple fact that neither are "new" states, but grow out of an ancient and proud nation that began its modernization a century ago, not just in the postwar period.

7

Foreign Relations

Thirty years after the Korean War ended, the two Koreas still face each other across a bleak demilitarized zone (DMZ), engaged in unremitting, withering, unregenerate hostility. Loudspeakers on both sides blare out bitter vilification around the clock. Armies of about 600,000 soldiers each are ready to fight at a moment's notice. The policy sequence in 1945–53 discussed earlier—from the early postwar internationalism to containment to rollback and then back to containment—meant that the Korean War really solved nothing, but it did solidify armed bulwarks, which the United States, the ROK, and the DPRK remain deeply committed to three decades after the war ended. Both Koreas continue to be deformed by the necessity to maintain this unrelenting struggle. Yet around the peninsula so much has changed.

For a quarter century after 1945, big-power strategic logic derived from the peninsula's promontory position in a world-ranging conflict. The fault lines bisected Korea; this small nation moved from the periphery to the center of the cold war because its hot war began at the point where two blocs intersected. The United States and 15 allied nations fought with South Korea; China fought with North Korea, and was backed by the U.S.S.R. and its other allies. The North Koreans sought to roll back the

South Koreans, and the United States sought to roll back the North Koreans, and the failure of both in 1953 froze a global conflict at the DMZ where it remains today.

Until the past decade there was little momentum to alter the situation. In the 1960s some people suggested major changes in American policy, among them Senator Mike Mansfield (D-Mont.), who called for Korea's demilitarization and neutralization. The ROK began actively supporting American policy, particularly with its dispatch of troops to fight in the Vietnam war (a total of more than 300,000 Korean soldiers eventually served there). The DPRK's actions ranged from offering new unification policies (such as its call for a confederation in 1960) to hostile acts along the DMZ and against the United States (such as the seizure of the spy ship *Pueblo* in 1968).

Watershed changes in world politics by the 1970s seemed to empty the cold-war logic of its previous meaning. With the emergence of the Sino-Soviet conflict, North Korea lost its joint backing. With the Nixon opening to China, both North and South Korea watched helplessly as their great-power benefactors cozied up to each other and changed the calculus of strategy: Would the United States or China again intervene in a war in Korea if that intervention would destroy the new Sino-American relationship? Given the overriding importance of the gains both powers made vis-à-vis the Soviet Union by virtue of their new-found friendship, many thought the answer had to be no. With the ending of the Indochina War in 1975, obstacles to ending the cold war throughout Asia were even fewer.

A Brief Thaw

The new strategic logic of the 1970s had an immediate and beneficial impact on South Korea. The Nixon Administration withdrew a division of American soldiers without heightening tension; the North Koreans responded by virtually halting attempts at infiltration (compared to 1968 when more than 100 soldiers died along the DMZ) and by significantly reducing their defense budget in 1971. In what seemed to be a miraculous development, both Koreas held talks at the highest level (between the director of

During the brief thaw in relations between the two Koreas in 1972, delegations from the ROK (left) and the DPRK exchanged documents at a Red Cross conference on family reunification.

the KCIA and Kim Il Sung's younger brother) in early 1972, culminating in a stunning July 4, 1972, announcement that both would seek reunification peacefully, independently of outside forces, and with common efforts toward creating a "great national unity" that would transcend the many differences between the two systems. Within a year this initiative had effectively failed, but it should never be forgotten as a reminder of what might be accomplished through enlightened and magnanimous diplomacy, and of the continuing importance of the unification issue.

American and Chinese policy also shifted, if less dramatically. By the end of the 1970s China had a significant indirect trade with South Korea, mainly through Hong Kong. China encouraged Pyongyang to take the path of diplomacy and restrained its more aggressive impulses. Henry A. Kissinger, then national security adviser, revealed in his memoirs that Kim Il Sung was in Beijing during Kissinger's famous "secret visit" in July 1971;

although it is not known if they met, it is likely that Nixon and Kissinger encouraged South Koreans to talk with North Koreans and indicated to them various benefits that might come their way if they continued on the moderate path. Kissinger pursued a plan for four-power talks to resolve tensions on the Korean peninsula, something that the North Koreans resisted because it suggested that outside powers would again decide Korea's fate.

When the Carter Administration announced plans for a gradual but complete withdrawal of U.S. ground forces from South Korea (air and naval units would remain deployed in or near Korea), the most prolonged period of North Korean courting of Americans began. Kim referred to President Jimmy Carter in 1977 as "a man of justice," and the DPRK press dropped its calumny against the United States, including the use of the term "U.S. imperialism." Kim gave interviews saying he was knocking on the American door, wanted diplomatic relations and trade, and would not interfere with American business interests in South Korea once Korea was reunified. The North Koreans also began using a term of opprobrium for Soviet imperialism, "domination-ism," a term akin to the Chinese usage, "hegemonism"; the DPRK seemed willing to enter, informally at least, an array (not an alliance, of course) of anti-Soviet states in Northeast Asia if it could get American trade and relations out of the deal. By and large Pyongyang stayed close to the Chinese foreign policy line during the Carter years, while taking care not to antagonize the Soviets needlessly. When Vietnam invaded Cambodia in 1978 the North Koreans forcefully and publicly condemned it, while maintaining a studied silence when China responded by invading Vietnam. For this act, some observers think, the Soviets temporarily shut off oil supplies to Pyongyang.

South Korean Initiatives

The South Koreans also moved quickly in the 1970s to exploit the new opportunities. They pursued an active diplomacy toward China and the Soviet Union and various East European countries, saying they would favor trade and diplomatic relations with "friendly" Communist regimes. They sought to shore up their support in the United States by cultivating congressional and Pentagon supporters, such as General John K. Singlaub, who denounced the proposed U.S. troop withdrawal and was fired for it by President Carter. The ROK built up strong support in the Middle East by dispatching thousands of construction workers; they also recycled petrodollars in this manner. At a less obvious level Seoul competed fiercely with Pyongyang to be the beneficiary of Sino-American détente and sought (sometimes successfully) to drive wedges between China and North Korea.

The disorders in South Korea in 1979–80, along with the regime change, brought an abrupt halt to all this new diplomacy. The Carter Administration dropped its program of troop withdrawal, arguing that North Korea had built up its ground forces by more than 200,000 in the mid-1970s. Since the United States has never made public the information upon which these new estimates were based, it is impossible to say whether it was this buildup, or fears for the stability of South Korea, that ended the withdrawal program. Perhaps it was both. In the author's view, the North Korean armed forces are no longer terribly formidable, given their obsolescent equipment. For example, the Soviets have never sold them MIG-23s or MIG-25s, which have been shipped to countries like Syria and Libya; the DPRK air force is therefore of late 1950s vintage, and the same would apply to its navy and much of the army's equipment. In general, there is an extraordinary degree of misinformation about the military balance on the peninsula. It seems to this writer that the balance has shifted decidedly in favor of South Korea in recent years, but that is denied by official spokesmen of the ROK and the United States, who continue to argue that the North Korean army is capable of overwhelming South Korea unless America helps. In any case, the unfortunate result of the 1970s was that several hopeful developments and apparent opportunities for enlightened diplomacy came to naught.

The Reagan Administration invited Chun Doo Hwan to visit Washington as its first foreign policy act, something also designed to bolster ROK stability. This earned an immediate virulent censure from Pyongyang. In the summer of 1981 Sino-American relations entered a difficult period, and DPRK-American relations correspondingly entered a period of deep freeze. For two years North Korea denounced the United States with all the considerable rhetorical forces at its command, and the United States committed itself to a modest but significant buildup of men and equipment in South Korea. Some 1,600 soldiers were added to the 40,000 Americans already there, advanced F-16 fighters were sold to Seoul, and, starting in 1979, huge military exercises involving upward of 200,000 American and Korean troops were held toward the beginning of each year. The Reagan Administration also developed a five-year Defense Guidance which suggested that were the Soviets to attack in the Persian Gulf, the United States might respond by "horizontal escalation," that is, attacking at a point of its own choosing. North Korea was such a point, the document said. This scenario truly horrified the North Koreans.

Sino-American relations warmed considerably in late 1983 and early 1984, leading to a new breakthrough on Korea. For the first time China said publicly that it wished to play a role in reducing tension in Korea; this was followed by a major DPRK initiative in January 1984 which called, for the first time, for three-way talks between the United States, the ROK and the DPRK. Previous to this the DPRK had never been willing to sit down with both at the same time. It was an initiative that the State Department seemed to welcome, terming it new and significant.

It may be that 1984 will witness some progress in moving the logjam in Korea or, more properly, melting the glacier. In any case, the same logic that stimulated the breakthroughs in the early 1970s remains valid today. None of the great powers sees profit in conflict on the Korean peninsula, none would like to be involved in a new war, and so the fault lines no longer cut across Korea.

U.S. Policy: Time for a Change

What might be a reasonable Korea policy for the United States? The State Department, the ROK, and many private observers argue that the existing Korea policy has worked to hold the peace since 1953, and that therefore the status quo is

ROK President
Chun Doo Hwan
visited Washington
two weeks after
President Reagan's
inauguration in 1981.

preferable: continued American troop commitments to South
Korea and continued support for it in its struggle with North
Korea. If North Korea does not give evidence of significant
change, they argue, how can we not assume the worst, that it is
still committed to the armed unification of the peninsula? Furthermore, if change is to come, it should involve all the great
powers concerned with Korea. Therefore in the past decade there
have been frequent calls for three-power, four-power, even
six-power talks to reduce tensions in Korea, or to arrange for
mutual cross recognition of both Koreas by all the powers. In the
early 1980s it also has been publicly acknowledged by the Chun
government that the ROK is Japan's first line of defense; this has
been since 1953 a powerful but usually unvoiced stimulus behind
the U.S. commitment in Korea.

It would seem, however, that new initiatives might be in order, since the above-mentioned ones have not proved successful. In the view of this author, the beginning of wisdom is to recognize that the United States bears the greatest responsibility for peace on the Korean peninsula and, in many ways, for failing to resolve the Korean conflict some 40 years after it began. Nowhere else in the world does the United States back one side of a conflict so exclusively, refusing to talk to the other side. Nowhere else does the United States directly command the military forces of another sovereign nation, as it continues to do in Korea. Therefore it would seem appropriate if the United States were to take the initiative by drawing down and eventually ending its troop commitment in South Korea, opening talks and trade with North Korea while continuing to support South Korea, encouraging China and Japan to move toward equidistance in their treatment of both Koreas, and pursuing every diplomatic and political means toward reducing the frightfully high levels of tension that still remain. In this manner the deep but by now anachronistic American direct involvement in Korea could be brought slowly to a close, a new and mutually beneficial relationship with both Koreas could evolve, and in any case Korea could again return to itself and to its region, moving as it has for millennia in the orbit of East Asia.

Talking It Over

A Note for Students and Discussion Groups

This issue of the HEADLINE SERIES, like its predecessors, is published for every serious reader, specialized or not, who takes an interest in the subject. Many of our readers will be in classrooms, seminars or community discussion groups. Particularly with them in mind, we present below some discussion questions—suggested as a starting point only—and references for further reading.

Discussion Questions

The author suggests that a number of traditional legacies are still influential in contemporary Korea. Give examples and tell how they might affect political systems as different as those in South and North Korea.

What role did the family play in Confucian societies? Did this affect the government or international relations, and if so, how?

Korea has a remarkable ethnic, linguistic, and historical unity. How has this affected nationalism? With such a background, why should Korea remain divided?

Since Japan helped to develop the Korean economy, why should there be such enmity between Koreans and Japanese? How can an economy be both <u>over</u>developed and <u>under</u>developed?

What effects did the colonial period have on Korea after 1945?

How did these effects make the U.S. occupation easy or difficult?

How was it that Korea came to be divided in 1945? Could this outcome have been avoided? From when would you date the emergence of the two separate regimes?

The author terms the Korean War a civil war. What are the reasons for this? What are the civil aspects of the war? What role did external powers play in the Korean War?

What effect did the Chinese involvement in the Korean War have? Is the North Korean-Chinese relationship new, or can one see traditional aspects to it?

What are some differences between the Rhee and Park periods in South Korea? How did each see the role of the state in the economy? Were there differences in how each related to the United States?

Kim Il Sung has been in power longer than almost any world leader. How do you account for this? What are the reasons for his longevity? What do you think will happen when he passes from the scene?

How would you describe North Korea's relations with the Soviet Union and China? Which model, the Soviet or the Chinese, has been more influential in the DPRK? How would you describe the unique features of the DPRK, when compared to China or the U.S.S.R.?

What is the Juche idea? Is it a Marxist idea? What does it suggest for Koreans at home, and for Korea's position in the world?

What are the reasons for the ROK's economic success in export-led development? Are there obstacles to this sort of development? What has been the impact of this new program on South Korean politics?

Can you come up with a formula for peaceful reunification in Korea? What would be a good policy to end the deadlock on the peninsula? Who should play a role in lessening tensions in Korea: The Koreans themselves? The United States? Three powers? Four powers?

Is the South Korean-American relationship likely to endure in its present form, or can you see changes around the corner?

READING LIST

Baldwin, Frank, ed., *Without Parallel: The American-Korean Relationship Since 1945.* New York, Pantheon Books, 1974. Critical and insightful essays on a number of postwar issues, including the UN and Korea, the ROK economy, and the failure of democracy in South Korea.

Cumings, Bruce, *The Origins of the Korean War: Liberation and the Emergence of Separate Regimes.* Princeton, N.J., Princeton University Press, 1981.

————, ed., *Child of Conflict: The Korean-American Relationship, 1943-1953.* Seattle, University of Washington Press, 1983.

Henderson, Gregory, *Korea: The Politics of the Vortex.* Cambridge, Mass., Harvard University Press, 1968. Excellent political history of Korea in modern times, combined with a theory of Korean society emphasizing centralization and a "vortex" process that is close to mass society theory.

Kihl, Young Hwan, *Politics and Policies in Divided Korea.* Boulder, Colo., Westview Press, 1984. The most-up-to-date survey of postwar Korean politics.

Kim, Key-Hiuk, *The Last Phase of the East Asian World Order: Korea, Japan and the Chinese Empire 1860-1882.* Berkeley, University of California Press, 1980. The best study of Korea's traditional foreign relations, and the end of the Sinocentric world order.

Kim, Se-jin, *The Politics of Military Revolution in Korea.* Chapel Hill, University of North Carolina Press, 1971. Useful study of the origins and leading figures of the South Korean military.

Kuznets, Paul W., *Economic Growth and Structure in the Republic of Korea.* New Haven, Conn., Yale University Press, 1977. The best single study of the South Korean economy.

Lee, Chong-Sik, *The Politics of Korean Nationalism.* Berkeley, University of California Press, 1963. The standard political history of the subject.

Lee, Mun Woong, *Rural North Korea Under Communism: A Study of Sociocultural Change.* Houston, Tex., Rice University Special Studies, 1976. An excellent study of collectivized agriculture in the DPRK.

Mason, Edward S., *et al.*, *The Economic and Social Modernization of the Republic of Korea.* Cambridge, Mass., Harvard University Press, 1980. The summary volume of a major study of the South Korean economy.

Palais, James B., *Politics and Policy in Traditional Korea, 1864–1876.* Cambridge, Mass., Harvard University Press, 1976. By far the best study of the Yi Dynasty. The author has a thorough command of the extensive primary sources, and provides a learned analysis of Korea's agrarian bureaucracy, the land system, the opening of Korea, and many other subjects.

Scalapino, Robert, and Lee, Chong-Sik, *Communism in Korea.* 2 vols.: *The Movement* and *The Society.* Berkeley, University of California Press, 1972. The most thorough treatment of North Korea.

Suh, Dae-Sook, *Korean Communism 1945–1980: A Reference Guide to the Political System.* Honolulu, The University of Hawaii Press, 1981.

————, *The Korean Communist Movement, 1918–1948.* Princeton, N.J., Princeton University Press, 1967. The first study to use the extensive collections of Japanese police reports on Korean communism, this is a standard work and comes with a companion volume of valuable documents.

Weinstein, Franklin B., and Kamiya, Fuji, eds. *The Security of Korea: U.S. and Japanese Perspectives on the 1980s.* Boulder, Colo., Westview Press, 1980. A good survey of peace and security in and around Korea.